Warrior • 124

Teutonic Knight

1190–1561

David Nicolle • Illustrated by Graham Turner

First published in Great Britain in 2007 by Osprey Publishing,
PO Box 883, Oxford, OX1 9PL, UK
PO Box 3985, New York, NY 10185-3985, USA
Email: info@ospreypublishing.com

Osprey Publishing is part of the Osprey Group.

A CIP catalogue record for this book is available from the British Library

ISBN: 978 1 84603 075 8

Page layout by Mark Holt
Index by Alison Worthington
Maps from the author's collection
Typeset in Helvetica Neue and ITC New Baskerville
Originated by United Graphic Pte Ltd, Singapore
Printed in China through World Print Ltd.

13 14 15 16 17   16 15 14 13 12 11 10 9 8 7

The Woodland Trust
Osprey Publishing is supporting the Woodland Trust, the UK's leading
woodland conservation charity, by funding the dedication of trees.

www.ospreypublishing.com

Artist's note

Readers may care to note that the original paintings from
which the colour plates in this book were prepared are
available for private sale. All reproduction copyright
whatsoever is retained by the Publishers. All enquiries
should be addressed to:

Graham Turner
PO Box 568
Aylesbury
Buckinghamshire
HP17 8ZX
UK
www.studio88.co.uk

The Publishers regret that they can enter into no
correspondence upon this matter.

Dedication

In memoriam August Auys, Royal Naval bandsman 1873–77
and mysterious ancestor.

Glossary

Balleien	(German) bailiwicks, administrative provinces of the Teutonic Order and other governing authorities.
camilis	(Latin) white garment worn by brethren of the Teutonic Knights.
Deutschmeister	(German) senior official in command of the Order's bailiwicks within the German Empire.
Diener	(German) servants.
Dienstherren	(German) ministerial 'lords of service'.
Dienstmänner	(German) ministerial 'men of service'.
Graumäntler	(German) 'those with grey mantles or cloaks', name given to *halb-brüder* (q.v.).
Halb-bruder	(German) literally 'half-brother', equivalent to brother-sergeants (see also *Graumäntler*).
Hochmeister	(German) Grand Master.
Komtur	(German) commander.
Komtureis	(German) commandery under the authority of a *komtur* (q.v.).
Landmeister	(German) governor of a large Teutonic Knights' province.
Marschall	(German) marshal.
ministerialis	(Latin) soldier of theoretically 'unfree' status.
Ritter	(German) 'horseman', usually translated as 'knight'.
Ritterschaft	(German) aristocratic 'knightly class'.
Sweik/Schweike	(German) Baltic breed of small horse.
Tresslerbuch	(German) literally 'Treasurer's Book'; financial accounts.

CONTENTS

TEUTONIC KNIGHT 1190–1561

INTRODUCTION

The background to the formation of the *Deutscher Orden* or Teutonic Order was the Third Crusade (1189–92), the effort by the three most powerful monarchs of Catholic Western Europe to regain Jerusalem. The crusade was only a partial success. Jerusalem was not retaken, but the 'Crusader' Kingdom of Jerusalem was re-established along the coast of Palestine and Lebanon, with the great port-city of Acre as its capital. For the German Imperial participants, however, this Third Crusade was a disaster, with Emperor Frederick Barbarossa dying before even reaching the Holy Land and a mere remnant of the great Imperial army arriving to take part in the siege of Acre. Amongst them were the men who established a field hospital, dedicated to the Virgin Mary, during that siege.[1]

There had been a German hospital in Crusader-ruled Jerusalem early in the 12th century, but there was no link between this and the German hospital founded during the Third Crusade. In March 1198 the new

'Angels lead a Christian army against infidels', a 15th-century German panel painting by the Master of the Legend of St Barbara. (Westfälischer Landesmuseum für Kunst und Kulturgeschichte/ permanent loan: Westfälischer Kunstverein, Munster)

1. See Osprey Campaign 161, *The Third Crusade 1191.*

hospital was granted Papal recognition as an independent military order, the *Fratres Domus hospitalis sanctae Mariae Teutonicorum* (Brethren of the German Hospital of St Mary), the organization that would become better known as the Teutonic Knights. Such recognition may have resulted from the efforts of the German Imperial Chancellor, Conrad von Querfurt, and thereafter the Teutonic Knights remained close to Imperial policies even when this caused tensions with the Papacy.

Although never as rich nor as influential as the largely French Order of Templars or the more mixed Hospitallers,[2] the Teutonic Knights acquired lands within the Crusader States (in the Middle East, but mostly in the Kingdom of Jerusalem), and established a military presence within the Armenian Kingdom of Cilicia, their ally. The Order's most important site was the fortress of Montfort in northern Palestine, which became its headquarters. In 1244, however, this new order of crusading knights suffered a devastating blow at the battle of La Forbie near Gaza, when the Kingdom of Jerusalem was defeated by the Ayyubid sultan of Egypt. Of the 400 Teutonic Knights present, 397 were killed, with the Templars and Hospitallers suffering almost as badly. Jerusalem, which had recently been regained by treaty, was lost again and in 1271 Montfort fell to the new Mamluk rulers of Egypt and Syria. Although the headquarters of the German Order were subsequently transferred to Acre, this defeat effectively marked the end of the Teutonic Knights' power in the Middle East.

Meanwhile, the Teutonic Order had continued to play a significant role in Cilicia, where their presence may have been encouraged by the Armenian rulers as a counterweight to the Templars, who were powerful in neighbouring Antioch. In addition to learning useful diplomatic and political skills there, the Teutonic Knights also held two important fortresses in the east of the Cilician state. These remaining Middle Eastern endeavours came to a halt with the fall of Acre in 1291.[3] However, there was already a faction within the Order that wanted to concentrate on expanding their power in the more promising arena of the Baltic. Conrad von Feuchtwangen was elected *Hochmeister* (lit. 'grand master') after the fall of Acre, and the Teutonic Knights' headquarters were re-established in Venice, rather than in Cyprus like the rival Templars and Hospitallers, perhaps as a compromise between those within the Order favouring the Middle East and those favouring the Baltic, where the Teutonic Knights were already deeply involved. (Those arguing in favour of the Baltic eventually got their way when the Order's headquarters were moved to Marienburg in Prussia in 1309.)

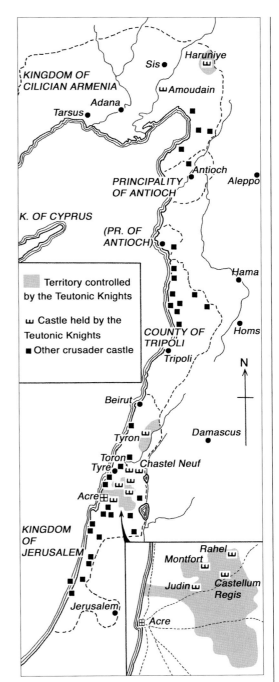

The Teutonic Knights in the Middle East.

---

2. See Osprey Warrior 91, *Knight Templar 1120–1312*; Warrior 33, *Knight Hospitaller [1] 1100–1306*; Warrior 41, *Knight Hospitaller [2] 1306–1565*.
3. See Osprey Campaign 154, *Acre 1291*.

'Guards at the Holy Sepulchre', one wearing a coat-of-plates that buckles at the back. Carving, late 13th century. (*In situ* cathedral, Mauritius Rundkapelle, Constance; author's photograph)

Hungary and Transylvania

The Teutonic Order already had experience of operating on another frontier within the non-Christian world, having served in early 13th-century Hungary. At this time Hungary was a rapidly evolving military state, with Magyar tribal armies who had created the state in the 10th century supported by nomadic or semi-nomadic refugees from the Eurasian steppes. But Hungarian kings also encouraged 'Westerners' to settle, to bolster the feudal army that they were creating. Since the mid-12th century Germans had also been encouraged to colonize south-eastern Transylvania, a rather primitive and almost autonomous region in what is now eastern Hungary and western Rumania.

Quite who inhabited Transylvania when King Andrew II of Hungary invited in the Teutonic Knights is still a matter of heated and all too often nationalistic debate. The normal Rumanian view is that the Vlachs, Latin-Rumanian speaking ancestors of the Wallachians and others, had been there since Roman times. Others maintain that the Vlachs migrated from farther south to live alongside Magyar-Hungarians, German settlers and others. Meanwhile, the population of neighbouring Wallachia was remarkably mixed during this period, consisting of Vlachs, Slavs and Turks, both Pecheneg and Kipchaq. Between Transylvania and Wallachia rose the Carpathian mountains which are, even today, amongst the wildest and least developed parts of Europe. Until the area was overrun by the Mongols in 1241, the politically and militarily dominant Kipchaq Turks – known to most medieval Europeans as Cumans – lived amongst Vlachs, who were tribally organized and almost as nomadic but largely Orthodox Christian. Christianity was also spreading amongst the Kipchaqs.

The Teutonic Knights arrived in this racially and religiously diverse Transylvania only seven years after the Fourth Crusade (1201–04) had conquered the Byzantine capital of Constantinople in 1204, raising hopes that a 'Latin' or Catholic 'Empire of Romania' (not to be confused with the modern state of Rumania) could be established in its stead. Perhaps King Andrew saw this volatile situation as an opportunity to back the still relatively minor Teutonic Order in preference to the wealthy and powerful Templars and Hospitallers. Having been invited into the small but strategically sensitive Burzenland or *Terra Borza*, the Teutonic Knights were encouraged to take control of the mountain passes and establish some sense of authority. Unfortunately, the Teutonic Knights exceeded their jurisdiction by erecting stone rather than timber fortifications. This action implied a more permanent military presence, a threatening prospect to King Andrew who was also facing resistance from a powerful group of his own barons. In 1225 he expelled the Teutonic Knights and

Bronze aquamanile in the form of a huntsman with a shield. The strong oriental influence seen in the tame hunting animal on the horse's back could indicate that it was made in late 12th-century Hungary. (Hermitage Museum, St Petersburg; author's photograph)

although the German Order felt that it had been ill-used, it had learned that to establish a territorial powerbase of its own it needed new territory which it had conquered for the Church and itself.

The Baltic, Poland and Russia

Having been expelled from the Burzenland in Hungary, and with other military orders dominant in the Middle East, the Teutonic Knights turned their attentions towards the Baltic where they would enjoy a freer hand. The Emperor offered encouragement but was too distant to exert his theoretical rights. The Pope was even farther away and enjoyed hardly more influence than the Emperor. When Duke Conrad of Mazovia asked the Teutonic Knights for their help against the pagan Prussians, the Order's *Hochmeister* agreed only on condition that the duke surrendered his rights in a small frontier territory around the settlement of Kulm. This provided the Teutonic Knights with an independent base from which to operate. Even so, the Order was not immune from the conflict between Pope and Emperor, which was reflected in tensions amongst the brethren until 1250. There was also continued competition for resources between those favouring the Middle Eastern and those supporting the Baltic campaigns.

The Teutonic Knights in Romania.

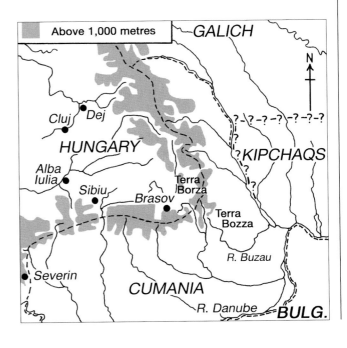

Effigial slab of a crusader knight from the chapel of Holm castle dating from the late 12th century, the earliest known image of a knight from territory that was subsequently ruled by the Teutonic Knights. (Latvian National Museum, Riga)

An engraved illustration of the castle and town of Ragnit, 17th century. (Staatsbibliothek Preussischer Kulturbesitz)

The medieval German Church had characteristics that set it apart from several of its neighbours. Most of its bishops were from the aristocracy and were themselves often competent military leaders, a characteristic that continued well into the 15th century. Many senior churchmen were significant land holders and formed part of the territorial aristocracy of the German Empire. In 1226 Frederick II's authorization of the conquest of Prussia explained that the crusade against pagan Prussia fitted the ideology of the Imperial government, which was seen by its supporters as the 'proper religious and political protector of mankind until the end of time'. This was based upon a belief that Augustus Caesar had been authorized, at the time of Christ's birth, to ensure the salvation of mankind: 'Just as He (God) provided the sacred Roman Empire for the purpose of spreading the Gospel, so our administration is anxious to bring about not only the conquest but also the conversion of the heathen nations.' The Teutonic Knights would be the strong-arm of this German Imperial policy within Prussia, Poland and other Eastern European territories, whilst ultimately promoting the Order itself. The Knights began their campaign in Prussia in 1228.

The Lithuanians were one of the originally pagan peoples of the Baltic region who became targets of crusading aggression. Slav tribes in what are now north-eastern Germany and northern Poland were also targets, but these were largely drawn into the Catholic Christian fold at a relatively early date, before the Teutonic Knights appeared on the scene. Though the trading and raiding of these peoples attracted attention, it was their paganism that Latin Catholic Europe found intolerable. Orthodox Christian Russians to the east also wished to convert these 'last European pagans', but set about the task with considerably less ferocity. In fact, it has been suggested that the 14th-century Lithuanians remained almost 'pagans against their will' as a means of resistance against conquest by the Teutonic Knights. The subsequent adoption of Russian Orthodox Christianity by the peoples of eastern Lithuania was a further snub to the Teutonic Knights' efforts, whereas the peoples of western Lithuania remained pagan for longer.

The Russians also realized that their own locally dominant position was threatened by the arrival of Catholic Crusaders and relations worsened after the Fourth Crusade overthrew the Orthodox Christian Byzantine emperor in Constantinople. Then came the first Mongol invasion of Russia in 1223, repeated 14 years later. Conversely, the Mongol invasion gave impetus to the efforts of the Teutonic Knights, who wanted to secure Lithuania as a means of shoring up the defences of Christian Europe in the face of the Mongol Golden Horde. Apparently believing the Russians to be reeling from this onslaught, the crusaders of the Baltic region tried to impose the Latin Catholic rite on the Russian city of Novgorod, followed by a crusade that ended in defeat at the 'battle on the ice' at Lake Peipus in 1242.[4]

Another Slav state that had ambitions in the Baltic region was, of course, Poland. Duke Conrad of the effectively autonomous Polish region of Mazovia had

4. See Osprey Campaign 46: *Lake Peipus 1242*.

already tried to force the pagan Prussians into submission with the aid of a new Military Order called 'The Knights of the Service of God in Prussia', established at Dobrzyn and widely known as the 'Brothers of Dobrzyn'. The effort failed, however, and the Knights of Dobrzyn were soon replaced by the Teutonic Knights. Tensions between Poles and Germans increased during the 13th century and less than 100 years later the Teutonic Knights would be accused of trying to eradicate the Polish language within their territories.

Despite the Teutonic Knights' absorbing what remained of the military order of Sword Brethren (originally known as the Brethren of the Knighthood of Livonia, then more commonly as the *Swertbrüdere*) after 1238, their dreams of a coastal empire linking up with Swedish crusaders in Finland faded following the defeat at Lake Peipus. Thereafter the Knights in Livonia, conducting their own war on paganism, joined their brethren in Prussia in campaigns against the Lithuanian territory that effectively

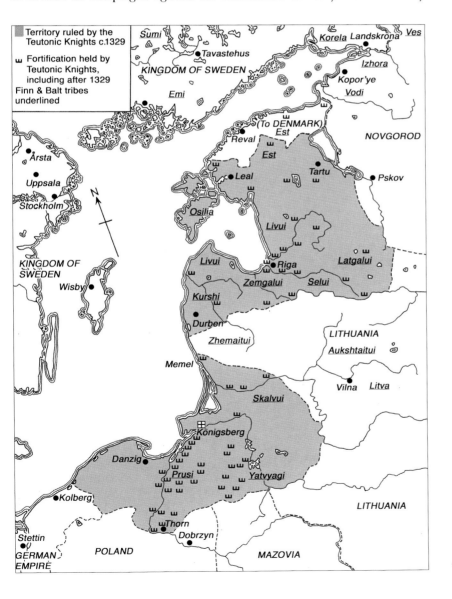

The Teutonic Knights in the Baltic.

The *Dansk* or latrine tower in the Teutonic Knights' castle of Thorn. (Stephen Turnbull)

separated their regions. (Cistercian monks had been active in Livonia since the mid-12th century, with the first Livonian Crusade launched in 1171.) In practical terms this separation remained until the end of the Teutonic Knights' authority in the Baltic. Nevertheless, the Teutonic Knights soon differed from other major military orders by becoming an order of warrior-monks forcefully ruling a commercial empire. Their Baltic state also had a profound impact upon crusading ideology during the 14th and 15th centuries. Paradoxically, however, Catholic Poland became a serious rival, eventually forming a union with the Teutonic Knights' traditional foes, the Lithuanians, whose conversion to Christianity in 1386 removed the Order's initial reason for existence in the Baltic area. These tensions came to a climax in 1410 when the Teutonic Knights were defeated at the battle of Tannenberg by an alliance of Lithuanians, Poles, Russians, Mongols and assorted mercenaries who had joined together to humble the increasingly arrogant Order.[5] The Teutonic Knights' state survived, but increasingly came to be seen as an anachronism.

A civil war within the Knights' Prussian Territories dragged on from 1454 until 1466; only Poland benefited from the resulting Peace of Thorn, with western Prussia coming under direct Polish rule while the *Hochmeister* ruled eastern Prussia as a Polish vassal. This arrangement had the strange effect of making the Teutonic Knights into crusaders once again when in 1485 they were drawn into low-level frontier warfare against the Ottoman Turks. A larger Polish campaign against the advancing Ottomans resulted in a major defeat for the Knights at Kozmin in western Ukraine in 1497. The Order in Livonia had remained outside Polish domination, but faced the growing might of Russian Muscovy and over the next 20 years the

5. See Osprey Campaign 122: *Tannenberg 1410.*

Reformation also undermined what remained of the Teutonic Order. In 1525 Albrecht von Hohenzollern-Ansbach, the last *Hochmeister* at Königsberg, declared Prussia to be a secular Duchy under Polish rule. A similar fate befell Livonia in 1561.

From establishing a small field hospital in Acre to being powerful rulers of Eastern European territories, the story of the Teutonic Knights takes us from the crusades in the Middle East to the battle for the souls of the last pagans of Europe. Originally formed to help re-conquer the Holy Land, the Knights' lasting legacy in history would be their crusading attempts within Europe itself and their efforts to carve out their own power base. Ultimately, however, there would be no place for this military order in the new Europe that was rapidly emerging.

CHRONOLOGY

1189–92	Third Crusade.
*c.*1190	Establishment of a German field hospital at the siege of Acre.
1191	German hospital established in Acre following the capture of the city.
1193	Pope Celestine III authorizes indulgences for crusaders in Livonia.
1196	Pope Celestine III grants the Brethren of the German Hospital the right to elect their own master.
1198	Brethren of the German Hospital reconstituted as the order of Teutonic Knights.
1199	Proclamation of the Livonian Crusade.
1209	Teutonic Knights start formulating their own customs.
1211	King Andrew II of Hungary gives the Teutonic Order the Burzenland frontier region.
1217–21	Teutonic Knights take part in Fifth Crusade in Egypt.
1221	Teutonic Knights are recognized as an independent international Order of the Church.
1225	Teutonic Knights are expelled from the Burzenland, but are invited to join the crusade in Prussia.
1226	*Hochmeister*s of the Teutonic Order receive the status of Imperial princes.
1227	Danish defeat at Bornhöved results in collapse of the Danish Baltic empire.
1228–29	Beginning of Teutonic Knights' conquest of Prussia.
1230	Teutonic Knights move headquarters to their new castle at Montfort.
1234	The Teutonic Knights' territory in Prussia becomes a Papal fief.
1236	Order of Sword Brethren is heavily defeated by Lithuanians at Saule.
1238	Abolition of Sword Brethren, whose remnants are incorporated into the Teutonic Knights.
1242	Army of Bishop Hermann of Estonia, Teutonic Knights and Danish allies defeated by principality of Novgorod at Lake Peipus; Prussians rebel against Teutonic Knights' rule.
1244	Separate rule of the Order of Teutonic Knights is recognized by the Pope.
1245	Teutonic Knights authorized to conduct a permanent crusade against the pagan Prussians.
1254	Crusade by King Ottokar II of Bohemia, Rudolf of Hapsburg and Otto of Brandenburg against Prussian pagans; foundation of Königsberg.
1260	Teutonic Knights defeated by Lithuanians at Durben; Prussians again rebel against Teutonic Knights.
1271	Teutonic Knights' headquarters-castle of Montfort falls to Mamluks.
1283	Teutonic Knights complete the conquest of Prussia.
1291	Acre falls to Mamluks; Teutonic Knights re-establish headquarters in Venice.

1308–09	Teutonic Knights acquire Danzig and eastern Pomerania.
1309	Teutonic Knights move their headquarters to Marienburg in Prussia, launching a permanent crusade against Lithuanian pagans.
1310	Papal investigation into Teutonic Knights in Livonia.
1346	Teutonic Knights purchase northern Estonia from the Danish king.
1386	Union of Poland and Lithuania; conversion of pagan ruler of Lithuania to Catholic Christianity.
1397	Teutonic Order's estates in Greece pay tribute to the Ottoman Turkish sultan.
1398–99	Teutonic Order agrees to help Lithuania against the Mongol Golden Horde; this alliance is defeated at Vorskla.
1410	Teutonic Knights defeated by Poland-Lithuania and their allies at Tannenberg.
1415–18	Council of Constance debates future of Teutonic Knights.
1457	Teutonic Knights move headquarters to Königsberg; the Order's estates in Prussia accept Polish overlordship.
1466	Autonomy achieved by *Hochmeister* of the Teutonic Knights in Livonia.
1483	Teutonic Order loses its estates in southern Italy.
1485	Teutonic Knights involved in warfare against Ottoman Turks in Wallachia (Rumania).
1492	Teutonic Order loses estates in Sicily.
1497	Major Teutonic Knights' campaign against Ottoman Turks in western Ukraine is defeated.
1500	Teutonic Knights lose last possessions in Greece to Ottoman Turks.
1501–02	Teutonic Knights of Livonia defeat Muscovite Russians near Lake Smolina.
1519–21	Teutonic Knights of Prussia defeated by Poland.
1525	Grand Master of the Teutonic Knights adopts Protestant Christianity and secularizes the Order in Prussia as a fief of Poland; Catholic Order of Teutonic Knights moves headquarters to Marienthal-Mergentheim in Germany.
1561–62	Secularization of the Teutonic Knights' territory in Livonia under Polish suzerainty.

A late 19th-century photograph showing the main 14th-century tower of the Teutonic Knights' castle of Königsberg. Much of the fortified wall and half-round to the right dated from 1482. (P. Campbell Collection)

ORGANIZATION

Organizationally, the Teutonic Knights had much in common with the Hospitallers and Templars. Their higher administration consisted of a General Chapter with representatives from each of the *Ballei* (bailiwicks; administrative provinces), five senior officers and the *Hochmeister*. The election of the *Hochmeister* was by an electoral college whose formation was complex but effective, beginning with the nomination of one brother knight as the 'election leader'. He then named another knight to join him; the two choosing a third and so on until 13 men had been selected. They were supposed to be widely representative of the Order, including brother sergeants.

The other senior officials of the German Order were the *Grosskomtur* (grand commander), the *Oberster Marschall* (supreme marshal), the *Oberster*

Spittler (supreme hospitaller), the *Oberster Trappier* (supreme draper) and the *Tressler* (treasurer). Even before the fall of Acre, the *Hochmeister* and Chapter in the Holy Land also usually appointed the *Deutschmeister*, who was in command of the Order's *Balleien* in Germany, as well as the *Landmeister*s (governors of large Teutonic Knights' provinces) of Prussia and Livonia. These *Landmeister*s had to send an annual report to the *Hochmeister* in Acre and every second or third year a brother went to render an account in person.

Of all the *Hochmeister*s of the Teutonic Knights, Hermann von Salza was regarded as the greatest, his statesmanship steering the Order through the bitter quarrels between Pope and Emperor in the early 13th century. During this period the Order also grew wealthy enough to launch its own military campaigns, including operations in the Baltic region. But it was only after the loss of their headquarters-castle of Montfort in 1271 that the faction which wanted the Order to focus its energies in the Baltic really became powerful. It was in these circumstances that the last *Hochmeister* in the Middle East, Burchard von Schwanden, resigned his command the year before Acre fell. The German master, Conrad von Feuchtwangen, who probably came to Acre with the 40 knights and around 200 other crusaders originally brought over by Burchard von Schwanden in 1289, was in command when the city actually fell.

The Teutonic Knights' main castles were not merely fortresses, but also served as administrative centres and monasteries where brethren led a communal religious life as 'warrior monks'. Each brother was subject to his local priory, the priories in turn being administered by the *Balleien*, which were answerable to the central administration of the Order, first at Acre or Montfort, then Venice, then Marienburg and Königsberg in Prussia. Within such a castle-convent was its commander, full brethren, *Halb-brüder* (half brethren) and usually a priest. The *Halb-brüder* were also distinguished by grey rather than white mantles, an appearance which gave them their other name of *Graumäntler*. Some took full monastic vows, but others who did not were allowed to marry and were usually allocated agricultural tasks. Then there were the *Diener* (servants) who formed part of an armed garrison, mostly crossbowmen and often operating as mounted infantry, and in the Middle East they were usually under command of a *Turcopolier*, who, as his name indicates, was in charge of the Turcopoles. The *Witinge* (indigenous Prussian freemen or nobles, now Christian) in many Baltic castles seem to have been Prussian freemen or nobles, whom the Teutonic Knights employed for special tasks. Finally, there were substantial numbers of non-combatants including craftsmen, wagoners and pack-horse handlers.

Although the Teutonic Knights became an international organization, their powerbase remained in Germany. Eventually they had 13 'houses' across the Middle East and Germany, with outposts in Cyprus, Greece, Calabria, Sicily, Spain, Flanders, Sweden and Hungary. Yet the Order's main centres would eventually be in Prussia, Livonia and Estonia. Records show that around 1250 there were 400 brethren in Palestine, 200 in other Mediterranean *Balleien*, 400 in the German *Balleien*, 400 in Prussia and 180 in Livonia.

Within Acre, before the walling of the suburb of Montmusard, there were six recognized 'quarters' – those of the Hospitallers, Templars, Pisa, Genoa, Venice and the Teutonic Knights. The last of these consisted of the

The 16th-century circular staircase between the 14th–15th-century *Marschallhaus* (right) and the late 16th-century Moskowiter Hall (left) of Königsberg castle, as it appeared in the early 20th century. (P. Campbell Collection)

eastern part of the walled city where the German Order purchased properties and tried to form them into a homogenous bloc. The Teutonic Knights may also have been given primary responsibility for the defence of the region immediately around the city and into Galilee. During the brief period when the Crusader Kingdom regained control of Jerusalem, the Order was given an area around the old hospital of St Marie des Allemands. The Teutonic Knights had few possessions in the other Crusader States of the Middle East, but in the Kingdom of Cilicia or Lesser Armenia they held the castles of Amoudain from 1211 until 1266 and Haruniye from 1236 until some time after 1271. These castles came with neighbouring *casals* or villages, which supplied revenues, food and perhaps labour. Furthermore, King Leon of Cilicia became a *confrater* (lit. 'fellow' or 'brother') or supporter of the Teutonic Knights and granted them freedom from sales

The Teutonic Knights' burial ground in Marienburg castle. (Photograph Stephen Turnbull)

and purchase taxes on victuals, necessities and horses. At one point the Order controlled four abbeys and 19 'rural domains' as well as the two castles, these being so important that a special capitular bailiff was appointed by the Grand Master. The Teutonic Knights always had a representative in the Papal Court to argue their case against bad news, rumours or accusations of religious deviation. They also played a significant role in the Hohenstaufen Kingdom of Sicily and southern Italy, reflecting their close but not always problem-free relationship with the Hohenstaufen German emperors.

The Teutonic Knights' foray into the frontier zone of Hungarian Transylvania in the early 13th century gave them control of the Burzenland. Dissatisfied with the defensive potential of the existing Pecheneg Turkish population against Kipchaq Turkish raids, King Andrew II invited the Teutonic Knights to occupy the area and erect five castles. They were supposed to be of traditional timber and earth construction, but recent archaeological work has confirmed what the documentary evidence claimed – namely that the Teutonic Knights used mixed stone and timber, presumably in opposition to King Andrew's wishes. Meanwhile, the area was colonized by settlers from several parts of Europe. After the Order won several skirmishes against the Kipchaqs,

The inner courtyard of Mewe castle. (Photograph Stephen Turnbull)

King Andrew donated additional territory in lands that Hungary did not really control, and also allowed the Teutonic Knights to build stone castles. At the same time the Order represented the Latin Catholic Church, which was already in competition with Orthodox Christianity in an area where the majority of the local Vlach population were Orthodox. The Teutonic Knights' ambitions and military activities in Transylvania came to an abrupt halt in 1225, the same year that the Order was invited to take part in a Crusade against the pagan Prussians.

During the early 14th century the Order had 12 *Balleien* within the Empire north of the Alps: Utrecht, Biesen, Coblenz, Lorraine, Alsace-Burgundy, Westphalia, Saxony-Thuringia, Hesse-Marburg, Franconia, Austria, Bohemia, all being under the *Deutschmeister*. There were, however, differences in the way the Order operated in the generally peaceful regions of western Germany when compared to the Baltic. In Franconia, for example, the Teutonic Knights had no influence within the local Church hierarchy, whereas the Order dominated those of Prussia and, to some extent, Livonia. The only significant possession that the Teutonic Knights held in Scandinavia seems to have been at Årsta, which was founded around 1260 near the Swedish coast. Far from being a city or major town, it was more like a large country farm.

Effigy of Hermann VIII of Henneberg-Römhild and his wife Elisabeth, made by the workshop of Peter Wischer, c.1510. (*In situ* parish church, Römhild)

In 1238 the Teutonic Knights absorbed what remained of the smaller German military order of the Sword Brethren which, prior to its defeat by the Lithuanians at Saule two years earlier, had consisted of about 110 knights, 400 to 500 mounted sergeants, about 700 mercenaries, 400 or so German vassals from its territories in Estonia, up to 5,000 native auxiliaries, six castles and numerous smaller outposts in Livonia. In Prussia the forests could be cleared and farmed well enough to provide financial revenues and food while an Imperial Bull of 1226 and a ducal 'deed of gift' four years later gave the Teutonic Knights much greater freedom of action across Prussia. After the division of Prussia into *Komtureis* (commanderies), each *Komtur* (commander) was the military and administrative chief of his area assisted by a 'convent' that theoretically consisted of 12 brother knights, each with a special role and title. Each *Komtureis* was supposed to provide 100 fighting men, including mercenaries, urban militias and native levies.

The Order's Baltic provinces were Prussia, itself consisting of the *Balleien* of Pomerelia, Prussia and Kulm, which was under direct rule of the *Hochmeister*, and Livonia, consisting of six convents inherited from the Sword Brethren, under a *Landmeister*. The administrative separation of Prussia and Livonia was regularized in 1243 with the official recognition of the Livonian commander as a *Vizelandmeister* (assistant *Landmeister*). Even after absorbing the remnants of the Sword Brethren, the Teutonic Knights in Livonia found themselves in competition with the powerful archbishop of Riga and other bishops, though the Order eventually emerged as the dominant force. Nevertheless, Livonia remained a loose federation of small feudal powers where the Teutonic Knights did not even control all the main fortresses.

The expansion of the Teutonic Knights' territory in the Baltic was not accomplished solely by conquering the indigenous pagans. They also inherited what previous crusaders and the Sword Brethren had gained. Some Hospitaller properties came to be Teutonic Knights' territory when the German Order expanded westward. In 1346 the king of Denmark sold his possessions in northern Estonia to the Teutonic Knights for 19,000 silver marks – about 4 tonnes (0.98 tons) of precious metal – and about 20 years later the Hospitallers sold their houses in Pomerelia to the Teutonic Knights. Yet even in 1380 there were still only around 700 Teutonic brethren in Prussia.

Castles and settlements

The Teutonic Knights' castles were essentially the same as those of other military orders. At Montfort in northern Palestine, for example,

archaeologists have not yet found evidence of stables, but there were cisterns, a kitchen and what appears to be a press for wine, oil or sugarcane. The chapel was probably on an upper floor of the central building, bits of stained glass and architectural fragments with painted heraldic motifs perhaps coming from its ceiling. The exact location of the Teutonic Knights' headquarters-convent in Acre has yet to be identified, but an account of the fall of Acre in 1291 by the anonymous Templar of Tyre stated that: 'The Germans also had a very lovely residence and a most noble tower, which was as large and lovely as that of the Temple.' The *Turris Alamanorum* was not attached to the eastern wall of the city, but may have commanded access to the port from the eastern gates.

ABOVE LEFT **A mid-14th-century wall painting of knights, formerly in Königsberg Cathedral and now in the Grünwald-Tannenberg Battlefield Site Museum. (Photograph Stephen Turnbull)**

ABOVE **The 14th-century Virgin's Tower of the Toompea castle, Talin. (Author's photograph)**

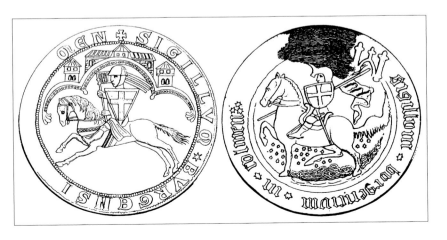

Seals of the city of Kulm under Teutonic Knights' rule: left – late 13th or early 14th century; right – c.1400.

17

The Teutonic Knights' castles and fortresses in the Baltic region are much better known, the first fortifications built by both the Teutonic Knights and the Sword Brethren reflecting the existing traditions of northern Germany as well as local Baltic styles. For example, during their initial conquest of Prussia, the Teutonic Knights erected simple earth and timber fortifications like those of their pagan foes. It was not until the later 13th century that major changes resulted in walled castles of stone or brick with rectangular plans, usually 50 to 60m (164 to 197ft) along the sides and with a central courtyard, and these became the typical 'convent castles' of the Teutonic Knights in the Baltic region. One of the most famous, but now sadly lost, was the *Schloss* of Königsberg (now Kaliningrad), which eventually became the Order's headquarters. Built in about 1257 on the site of a pagan Prussian fortress called the *Twangeeste*, the *Conventhaus* (conventual building containing living and other quarters) of half a century later was at the western end of the subsequent castle, but was demolished at a relatively early date. It had been surrounded by a courtyard, beyond which was a 13th-century wall with rectangular towers. These were again mostly replaced by round towers in the 14th and 15th centuries, plus a polygonal tower near the main gate.

'Colonial cities' became a feature of Germany's eastward expansion into Slav tribal territory. Those founded by the German military orders in the 13th-century Baltic region were essentially the same, usually built on a rectangular grid pattern which was used even where the terrain meant that the outer wall of the town was not rectangular in plan. Kulm, founded by the Teutonic Knights in 1232, was an example.

BELOW **Part of a collapsed cross-vault from Montfort castle, showing part of the painted arms of the *Hochmeister* of the Teutonic Knights. (Metropolitan Museum of Art, Gift of Clarence Mackay et al., inv. 1928.28.99.3, New York)**

BELOW RIGHT **The crenellated 14th- or 15th-century town hall of Talin, Estonia. (Author's photograph)**

Administration and trade

In addition to fighting, running medical hospitals, and providing hospitality to pilgrims, the sick and the old, the Teutonic Knights had huge administrative responsibilities, most obviously in their Baltic territories. The cost of warfare was enormous and so a reliable source of income was vital. Most of the Teutonic Knights' wealth was in Germany, but their castles in the Middle East and the Baltic were intended to raise local revenues where possible. In Prussia and Livonia the brethren almost inevitably became businessmen, trading in wheat, hides and wool on behalf of the Teutonic Order. In fact, at the height of the Teutonic Knights' power and wealth they were also involved in long-distance trade with the Middle East, the Balkans and Greece.

From the start of their campaigns of conquest and conversion in the Baltic, the Teutonic Knights encouraged colonization and economic development to maintain their finances and manpower. Colonization proved relatively easy because the region was close to Germany and some of the land was suitable – though swathes of forest and marsh were not. Settlers were given wide-ranging privileges, equivalent to the best that could be found in the towns of Germany, these being codified in the *Kulmer Handfeste* within three years of the Teutonic Knights conquering Kulmerland. The Order also waived its rights to many kinds of taxation and made feudal military service as light as possible, while trade was made easier by using a standard coinage. The Teutonic Knights were correspondingly enlightened in the regulations they laid down concerning the design of houses, working to avoid overcrowding and the ever-present threat of fire, and to handle the threat of pagan attack.

The major product of the Teutonic Knights' Baltic territories was wheat, but the area also produced horses, leather and wool, plus cattle and sheep for meat. Other products included lime and salt. The leather industry used local materials, but iron seems to have been imported from Hungary and Sweden. Industrial production was concentrated in the towns where the Order imposed strict control, especially on arms production and trade. This economic activity required financial controls on credit and the supervision of craft guilds, particularly those concerning wool, leather, wagons and glass. There was also a thriving transit trade through the Teutonic Knights' territory, some stemming

ABOVE LEFT **Königsberg castle in the mid-20th century, showing the polygonal 14th-century north-eastern tower and the original main entrance, greatly modified in 1532–33. (P. Campbell Collection)**

ABOVE **An early 20th-century photograph of the interior of the chapel of the castle of Königsberg, largely rebuilt in the 16th century. (P. Campbell Collection)**

'The theft of cattle', from an early 14th-century German legal manuscript from Soest. (*Nequambuch IV*, Stadtarchiv, A.2771, Soest, North-Rhine-Westphalia)

A 15th-century merchant's house in Talin, Estonia, including storage facilities and crane. (Author's photograph).

from generally unfriendly lands to the east. Overall, what might be called the 'state sector' brought the Order huge profits through agriculture, industry and trade. Though they varied, the revenues never dried up.

Diplomacy was central to the activities of every military order and the Teutonic Knights' business activities resulted in far-ranging diplomacy, reaching England, Sicily, Hungary and beyond. The Teutonic Knights were similarly cultivated by other powers, often concerning economic matters. For example, during a diplomatic tour of Germany to win the recognition of Henry IV as the new king of England, Sir William Sturmy went to Prussia to urge the *Hochmeister* to end an embargo on the importation of English cloth. In the mid-15th century the *Hochmeisters* of the Teutonic Knights were even involved in negotiations with Scotland, trying to settle trade disputes concerning the Hanseatic League port of Danzig. Over the centuries the Teutonic Knights' reputation for diplomatic skills resulted in a German proverb: 'If you're so clever, go and deceive the lords of Prussia.'

Early Priors and *Hochmeister*s of the Teutonic Order

Priors under the tutelage of the Hospitallers at Acre
Sibrand: 1190
Gerard: 1192
Heinrich: 1193–94
Ulrich: 1195
Heinrich (*praeceptor*, almost certainly Heinrich Walpot): 1196

***Hochmeister*s resident at Acre**
Heinrich Walpot: 1198–1200
Otto von Karpen: 1200–08
Heinrich Bart: 1208–09/10
Hermann von Salza: 1210–39
Anno von Sangershausen: 1257–74
Hartmann von Heldrungen: 1274–83
Burchard von Schwanden: 1283–90

***Hochmeister*s resident at Montfort**
Hermann von Salza: 1210–39
Conrad von Thüringen: 1239–40
Gerhard von Malberg: 1241–44
Heinrich von Hohenlohe: 1244–49

Gunther von Wullersleben: 1249–53
Poppo von Osterna: 1253–57
Anno von Sangershausen: 1257–74

***Hochmeister*s resident at Venice**
Conrad von Feuchtwangen: 1291–97
Gottfried von Hohenlohe: 1297–1303
Siegfried von Feuchtwangen: 1303–11

***Hochmeister*s resident at Marienburg**
Siegfried von Feuchtwangen: 1303–11
Karl von Trier: 1311–24
Werner von Orslen: 1324–31
Luther von Braunschweig: 1331–35
Dietrich von Altenburg: 1335–41
Ludolf von König: 1341–45
Heinrich Dusemer: 1345–51
Winrich von Kniprode: 1352–82
Conrad Zöllner von Rothenstein: 1382–90
Conrad von Wallenrode: 1390–93
Conrad von Jungingen: 1393–1407
Ulrich von Jungingen: 1408–10

Heinrich von Plauen: 1410–13
Michael Küchmeister: 1414–22
Paul von Russdorf: 1422–41
Conrad von Erlichshausen: 1441–49
Ludwig von Erlichshausen: 1450–67

***Hochmeister*s resident at Königsberg**
Ludwig von Erlichshausen: 1450–67
Heinrich Reuss von Plauen: 1469–70
Heinrich von Richtenberg: 1470–77
Martin Truchsess von Wetzhausen: 1477–89
Johann von Tiefen: 1489–97
Friedrich von Sachsen: 1498–1510
Albrecht von Hohenzollern-Ansbach: 1511–25 (thereafter holding Prussia as a Duchy of Poland).

***Hochmeister*s resident at Mareintal-Mergentheim (where the Order existed in a nominal form until 1809)**
Walter von Cronberg: 1527–43
Wolfgang Schutzbar Milchling: 1543–66

RECRUITMENT

Recruitment to the Teutonic Knights differed from that of other military orders largely because of the phenomenon of the *ministeriales* within the German Empire, these providing the majority of brother knights during the late 12th and 13th centuries. Furthermore, the Imperial *ministeriales* donated substantial properties to the Order, even if they did not join themselves. The Latin word *ministerialis* was usually translated into medieval German as *Dienstmann* (servant). By the first half of the 12th century the *ministeriales* were already a significant military force, but remained theoretically 'unfree' serfs. Of course few men in 12th-century Europe would have regarded themselves as 'free' in the modern sense, almost all being bound in some way. (To some extent the only really free or masterless man was the outlaw.) Similarly, their womenfolk were obliged to make and mend the *ministeriales*' clothing and some other equipment in return for their lords' 'compensating' them with foodstuffs.

Though legally still unfree, the *ministeriales* paradoxically came to be regarded as noblemen during the 12th century, increasingly living in castles, entitled to 'judgement by their peers' and indulging in personal feuds. This caused difficulties for their lords who were often amongst the 'Church Princes' who were a feature of medieval Germany. *Ministeriales* existed in other countries including France, but in 12th-century Germany they became a true 'aristocracy of service', though initially including both *Dienstmänner* (men of service) and *Dienstherren* (lords of service), the latter being in the first rank of Imperial public officials. Things changed during the 13th century, with ministerial 'knights' increasing in social prestige, while the *Dienstmänner* could still come from humble, artisan or even serf backgrounds. By the 14th century the aristocratic status of the German *ministeriales* was

Statue of Count Eckhart, a founder of the cathedral, and his wife, c.1249, which is one of a series of such statues in the cathedral of Naumberg. (Author's photograph)

generally accepted, their bonds of serfdom finally disappeared and many became an autonomous *Ritterschaft* or 'class of knights' within Imperial Germany's numerous territorial principalities.

It has been suggested that the concept of the knight had a more spiritual and overtly Christian content in Germany than in France or England during the 11th and 12th centuries. Nevertheless, the motives for joining the Teutonic Knights were similar to those of the other military orders and were not necessarily religious. Men could be escaping problems, seeking higher prestige or just looking for regular meals. From its inception the Order of Teutonic Knights welcomed all militarily capable recruits, nobles or otherwise, who were subjects of the German Emperor. Nor did they necessarily have to be Germans, especially in the early days, though aristocratic status subsequently became important. Such recruits had to answer ten questions, the first five with appropriate 'No' answers and the second five with 'Yes'. These were:

> Do you belong to another Order?
> Are you married?
> Have you any hidden physical deformity?
> Are you in debt?
> Are you a serf [other than a *ministerialis*]?
> Are you prepared...
> To fight in Palestine?
> Or elsewhere?
> To take care of the sick?
> To practise any craft you know, as ordered?
> To obey the Rule?

Next the new member made his 'profession': 'I .... do profess and promise chastity, renunciation of property, and obedience to God and to the Blessed Virgin Mary and to you, Brother .... Master of the Teutonic Order, and to your successors, according to the Rule and Institutions of the Order, and I will be obedient to you, and to your successors, even unto death.'

A remarkable amount is known about the origins of the brethren. Between 1250 and 1309 over 40 per cent of brothers and over 30 per cent of commanders came from Thuringia; almost 20 per cent of brothers and almost 30 per cent of commanders came from Saxony; almost 25 per cent of brothers and just over 25 per cent of commanders from southern Germany; almost 7 per cent of brothers and over 10 per cent of commanders from the Rhineland; and the remainder from elsewhere. Over 12 per cent came from the upper aristocracy, over 7 per cent from knightly families, over 75 per cent from the *ministeriales*, and over 4 per cent from other classes.

The limited surviving information about the recruitment and origins of the *Graumäntler* suggests that some came from German settler families within the Order's Baltic realm, or even from indigenous peoples, though the great majority were from Germany, being of much the same artisan and peasant origins as seen in the other military orders.

Considerably more is known about the background of senior men, four of the first 15 *Hochmeister*s being the sons of *ministeriales*, five the sons of knightly landowners, one the son of a middle-class burgher, one a territorial prince, and four unknown. It is also clear that brethren from the aristocracy progressed more quickly and had a much better chance of reaching high rank.

As in all the military orders, the Teutonic Knights were hugely dependent upon others who, though not brethren or even half-brethren, fought, worked or otherwise supported the Order. These included local auxiliaries from both the indigenous and settler communities within the Teutonic Knights' territories. Here some of the now Christian, Prussian native aristocracy had been 'Germanized' by the late 13th century, adopting Western European styles of warfare. Others, though converted to Christianity, clung to the old ways and did military service for the Teutonic Knights armed with 'Prussian weapons', indicating that they usually served as light cavalry. Though valuable against the pagan Lithuanians, they were not permitted to join the Order as brethren. Many native chiefs similarly fought for Teutonic Knights in Livonia and Estonia. Nevertheless, there was a gradual shift away from a general levy to the raising of a fixed quota of men from each *vakus* (small district in the Baltic). During the 15th century even these declined in importance, though the principle of a peasant militia role survived and was still used against Russian invaders in the 16th century.

Numerous settler knights held fiefs within the Teutonic Knights' Baltic territories and they, like the towns and the land-holding church, owed feudal military service. In 1236 the *Hochmeister* enfeoffed a knight in Prussia with a small castle, 300 'Flemish hides' (about 2,630 hectares/6,500 acres),

A drawing of the late 14th-century effigial slab of the Teutonic brother knight Kunos von Liebenstein, originally in the castle of Lochstedt. (After Steinbrecht)

Earthworks dating from the period of the Sword Brethren and the Teutonic Knights in the citadel of Tartu, Estonia. (Author's photograph)

The southern tower of Riga, which was originally the eastern tower of the Teutonic Knights' castle. (Photograph Stephen Turnbull)

plus the fisheries and tithes of three villages. In 1261 knights were offered 40 hides in Livonia, squires ten, and tithe exemption for six years in return for coming to fight against rebels. Though the secular aristocracy of Livonia often squabbled amongst themselves, a nobleman of German origin in the 14th century possessing at least 40 hides (1,944 hectares/4,803 acres) of land was supposed to serve in full armour with an armoured horse and at least two other cavalrymen. Those with 10 (486 hectares/1,200 acres) to 40 hides served with a *Platendienst* (coat-of-plates), and rode an inferior horse. By the early 15th century the Teutonic Knights were almost entirely dependent upon the *Wehrpflichtige* (local levies), which nominally consisted of 426 knights, 3,200 serving men, 5,872 sergeants, 1,963 troops provided by six great towns, and about 1,500 *Stiftsmänner* (men from territory held by the abbeys). Forces raised by various ecclesiastical authorities were clearly very important, but this could also cause difficulties, with competition for the limited available military manpower.

One significant source of fighting men that was effectively reserved for the Teutonic Order consisted of crusaders who volunteered to serve under its command. In fact, such crusaders were vital for any major offensive operations in the Baltic. Amongst them were some very senior men. The new city of Königsberg was named after King Ottokar II of Bohemia who fought against the Prussians in 1255, while King John the Blind of Bohemia (later killed at Crécy in 1346) fought alongside the Teutonic Knights on two campaigns. On the other hand, the mid-14th-century Austrian poet Heinrich der Teichner complained that knights only went to Prussia to waste money and win glory, neglecting their duties at home.

Men came from beyond the Empire as well, the senior Swedish nobleman Karl Ulfsson being killed at the battle of Durben in 1260. Others came from France and England, including Henry of Grosmont who went on crusade to Prussia and became renowned for piety as well as chivalry. Perhaps the most famous Englishman to fight alongside the Teutonic Knights was fictional – from Chaucer's *Canterbury Tales*:

There was a Knight, a most distinguished man,
Who from the day on which he first began
To ride abroad had followed chivalry,
Truth, honour, generousness and courtesy.
When we took Alexandria, he was there.
He often sat at table in the chair
Of honour above all nations when in Prussia.
In Lithuania he had ridden, and Russia,
No Christian man so often, of his rank.

The prestige of fighting alongside the Teutonic Knights was similarly reflected in the fact that the *Tierselet*, a confraternity of real fighting knights in late 14th-century Poitou in western France, adopted two forms of insignia for those who had been to Prussia: one for those who had merely gone there and another for those who had participated in combat against the heathen. During peace efforts in the later 14th century, Earl Henry of Derby tried to get safe conduct from the French king so that he could take part in the Duke of Bourbon's crusade against Islamic North Africa in 1390, but failing in this he went to Prussia with 300 or so followers. On the French side, the Sire de Boucicaut went to Prussia three times as a young man, joining Conrad von Wallenrod's campaign in 1391 where he 'saw it was a grand affair, and most honourable and fine.'

Mercenaries fought in the Baltic largely for financial reasons, large numbers of so-called Genoese crossbowmen being recruited in the late 14th and early 15th centuries. Some efforts were also made to recruit English bowmen, but not many arrived. Many men came from Germany, including gunners and other specialists in the new field of firearms. In fact, a growing reliance on mercenaries resulted in increased taxation throughout the Teutonic Knights' territory.

Like the other military orders, the Teutonic Knights soon employed lawyers, particularly because of their complicated dual allegiance to Emperor and Pope, and because they became rulers of huge domains in

The carved head of a 'knight' from the Teutonic Knights' castle of Montfort, 13th century. (Courtesy of the Israel Antiquities Authority)

the Baltic region. Some worked for the Teutonic Knights on a regular basis, including Master Accursus of Arezzo who was employed by the Order in the Kingdom of Jerusalem during the late 13th century. The Teutonic Knights also recruited law students; however only six of the 44 identified law students they subsidized were themselves members of the Order, most coming from the Order's territories in Prussia and Livonia.

BELIEF AND BELONGING

The life of a member of a military order was governed by that order's Rule. The Teutonic Knights largely copied the Hospitallers' Rule for charitable tasks, and the Templars for military duties, this first composite Rule of the Order of Teutonic Knights being 'granted' by the Pope in 1199. A separate and more distinctive Teutonic Rule was compiled by Cardinal William of Sabina before 1245, but many other regulations were added later. Translated in German in 1264, copies were kept in every *Komtureis*, where one section was explained each Sunday. Care of the sick and poor was, of course, regarded as part of the Teutonic Knights' spiritual life and was, according to the Rule, an expression of piety. When a sick person entered one of the Order's hospitals, he or she had to make their confession and receive the sacrament.

The brethren were governed by the Rules, Laws and Customs of the Order, the Rules being 'eternal chastity, renunciation of one's own wishes, that is obedience unto death, and the third is a vow of poverty.' All property was held in common and brethren were not even allowed to own private chests in which to keep clothes and other items. Laws laid particular emphasis on the Teutonic Knights' role as 'Christ's warriors' and also showed how brethren should avoid temptation, especially concerning women and homosexual practices. Possession of money and the exchange of any items issued for personal use were not allowed. Normal penalties for the infringement of Rules, Laws and Customs ranged from three days of penance to one year's hard labour working with the servants and deprivation of the Order's insignia. More extreme sentences, such as the burning alive of rebellious brethren, had to be authorized by the Pope.

The Teutonic Knights' religious liturgy had largely been copied from that of the Templars, but was further developed during the 13th century, for example, by adopting the Dominican Friars' routine of religious observances. Teutonic brethren thus received communion seven times a day, which could be difficult in the short daylight hours of a northern winter, whereas the Templars only received communion three times. No meat was eaten on Mondays, Wednesdays, Fridays, Saturdays and during Lent. There was a meatless season during most of November and December. Brethren had to make their confession to a priest of their own Order if one was available, and in fact brother priests had considerable spiritual authority over their lay brethren, though the latter took part in the punishment of a brother priest if he broke the Rule. Because the Order ruled a substantial part of north-eastern Europe, it was also responsible for Christianity amongst its subjects, and it had a profound impact upon spiritual as well as political and economic life in Prussia, though to a lesser extent in Livonia.

Warrior in combat with a serpent, German carved relief, c.1200. (*In situ* Church of St Michael, Altenstadt; author's photograph)

While the Church agreed that the Teutonic Knights could enslave non-Christian captives and fell the pagans' sacred oak trees, some elements of Baltic paganism survived for a time under their rule. Their largely pagan Lithuanian foes practised a policy of more overt religious toleration which did not, however, mean that they treated captured Teutonic Knights with special consideration. Captured men were often killed because they so easily escaped, whereas women and children were enslaved, sometimes for sale to slave traders. Captured Teutonic Knights were not always killed, of course, though their chances of survival and release were better in the Middle East than in the Baltic.

On the Christian side of the frontier, men were motivated by various means, including the legal fiction that fighting on crusade in the Baltic was a pilgrimage comparable to going to the Holy Land. Even so, there was evidence of growing reluctance amongst Teutonic Knights' brethren in Germany to be transferred to the Baltic, though service within a war-torn frontier zone or in the Order's headquarters-convent in Königsberg could enhance a man's prospects of promotion.

Religious motivation played a major role in the mindset of the Teutonic Knights, the cult of crusading martyrdom being highly developed in medieval German poetry. It was even suggested that such martyrs took the place of Lucifer's fallen angels in Heaven's 'tenth choir of angels'. This attitude probably accounted for a willingness to leave the dead where they lay, even if they were Christians from one's own side. Those who died in a Holy War had gone to heaven, so their bodies were not important.

Morale was also maintained through a cult of the Virgin Mary and various saints, the *Officium Marianum* (Service of Mary) being said daily in addition to the usual church services, while one of the most important literary works produced by the Teutonic Order was *The Passional*, which recounted the life of the Virgin and her miracles. The Teutonic Knights also adopted St George and St Elizabeth of Thuringia as their patrons, St George being particularly popular in Prussia. The significance of religious relics was clear in a number of battles, as when the Teutonic Knights' Marschall Dietrich von Bernheim led a daring night raid against the Pomeranian rebel-held town of Sartowitz on the night of 3 December

1241. His small force returned with one such sacred relic, the head of St Barbara, the night of the raid also being that of the feast of St Barbara.

The Teutonic Knights, like other crusaders and settlers in the Baltic region, frequently looked down upon the indigenous Finn and Balt peoples, even after the latter had converted to Christianity. Modern concepts of racism are probably inappropriate for the medieval period, yet the Teutonic Knights quite openly described their Prussian subjects as 'slaves of the Devil' who, since their conversion, were now 'slaves of Christ'. Meanwhile, the Teutonic Knights saw themselves, and were seen by others, as straightforward fighting men, an attitude summed up in a poem written to celebrate a Teutonic Knights' victory at Sirguna in 1234: 'Let us all show joy of heart, For lo, the heathen feel the smart.'

The most famous piece of Teutonic Knights' literature is, however, the *Livländische Riemchronik* or *Livonian Rhymed Chronicle*, written at the

St George and the Dragon, a painted panel showing typical German armour of the second half of the 15th century. (*In situ* Church of St George, Nördlingen, Bavaria)

end of the 13th century and probably based on oral traditions, although the author's knowledge of warfare suggests that he had some personal experience. It was probably intended to increase enthusiasm, support and volunteers by recounting the heroism of the Order, as in its description of the aftermath of the battle of Lake Peipus:

> Master Herman Balke was in conflict with the Russians
>   and heathens.
> He had to defend himself against both with great fighting,
> And thus combated these enemies of God.
> The bishop and the king's men (the Danes) agreed
> With all that he did, as the successes indicate …
> May God reward his great deeds with a heavenly crown!

Following the fall of Acre in 1291 there was a widespread decline in enthusiasm for crusading on all fronts, and this may have been the reason for the writing of Peter von Dusburg's *Chronicon Terre Prusse* (Chronicle of the Prussian Land) around 1330. It was intended to influence public opinion in favour of the Order's Baltic crusade and was translated into vernacular German ten years later as the *Krônike von Prûzinland*. Literacy was now spreading across Germany and this work may have been for public reading as well as private study. Other propagandists even identified the Biblical 'Four Horsemen of the Apocalypse' with the military orders of Templars, Hospitallers, Teutonic Knights and also the Militia Christi founded by St Dominic. The 13th-century English scholar Roger Bacon was less impressed, complaining that:

> the Christian princes who labour for their conversion [the pagans], and especially the brothers of the Teutonic Order, desire to reduce them to servitude… For this reason they offer opposition, hence they are resisting oppression, not the arguments of a superior religion.

Fatalism and defeatism became widespread amongst the Knights during the 15th century. On the other hand criticism came against the backdrop of a general anti-monastic feeling in later 15th-century Europe. An undated Estonian song similarly railed against their rulers' arrogance: 'Puff yourselves up, you Germans, thinking yourselves better than anyone else in the world, you dislike all that we poor Estonians do. May you be plunged therefore, into the depths of hell.' There could sometimes be an unexpected clash between religious and secular motivation within the knightly class. For example, German poetry about the crusades often expressed a spirit of magnanimity towards non-Christians that was lacking in official religious sources, the heathen warrior being described as an honourable but misguided opponent. Furthermore, the indiscriminate slaughter of the enemy was portrayed as a sin because Christian knights were supposed to emulate the mercy shown by God to His enemies. This was clear in Wolfram von Eschenbach's epic *Parzival*, completed during the first years of the 13th century. An even more remarkable plea for tolerance came from the hero's Saracen consort in von Eschenbach's *Willehalm* and based upon the idea that human beings, including infidels and heathen, had fallen from grace because of temptation whereas the fallen angels had done so because of their own free will.

APPEARANCE AND EQUIPMENT

In many respects the appearance of members of the Teutonic Knights went against the knightly, chivalric ethos from which its recruits were drawn, which regarded fine or decorated clothing, bright arms and armour and gilded horse-harness as proper for members of the military élite. The *habit* or uniform of the Teutonic Knights was specified in detail, all brothers wearing a black cross on their overtunics which, from 1244 onwards, were always white. That year the Pope allowed the clerics of the Order to wear white *camilis* over their other clothes, white having previously been the mark of a brother knight. 'Worldly splendour' was forbidden and no brother could possess more than the uniform kit consisting of two shirts, a pair of breeches, two pairs of 'boots' (in reality perhaps hose), a surcoat, a sleeping bag, a blanket, a breviary and a knife. A fur coat had to be of cheap goatskin or sheepskin. The men slept in their shirt, breeches and boots, and they were not permitted to lock the box in which they kept their clothing. They were allowed to wear a beard but their hair had to be short. Nor were they allowed to display their own coat-of-arms, if they had one, or to joust or hunt most forms of game. Their only lawful amusement was woodcarving. All 'courtesy and conviviality' with secular knights was forbidden.

'The Virgin Mary armed and attended by the Powers', on the *Altarpiece of Albrecht II* painted in 1438, showing an array of armour and weapons hanging on the wall. (*In situ* Klosterneuburg, Austria)

The bulk of the arms and armour used by the Teutonic Knights in the Baltic region was imported from elsewhere, largely from Germany where the main production centres were in the south and west of the country. One such German armour-making centre was Iserlohn, which as early as 1252 had an armourers' guild or *Panzergilde*, with St Pancras as its patron saint. By the mid-14th century Nürnberg had become a major centre of armour manufacture. In fact, the adoption of water power for wire-drawing to make mail was attributed to Rudolph von Nürnberg around 1350. By then virtually all German cities also had a permanently employed, officially recognized crossbow-maker who produced a specified number of these weapons every year, being paid extra for any additional crossbows. Some parts of Scandinavia soon also had flourishing crossbow-making industries, exporting to the Teutonic Knights on the other side of the Baltic Sea.

Military equipment was clearly made within the Teutonic Knights' territories, at least one captured craftsmen saving his life by showing the pagans how to make crossbows. In 1396, 7,000 crossbow bows of yew and 1,150 of *Knottelholcz*, which might mean composite construction, were sent from Ragnit to the *Hochmeister*. Three years later the Order's archives record the purchase of spanning hooks with belts and quivers inside Teutonic Knights' territory. Clearly, the larger towns within the Order's state had their own crossbow-makers, as well as separate craftsmen who mounted the bolt-heads on the shafts, made the fletching and so on, as was the case in Germany. In 1409 there were no fewer than 1,200 billy-goat horns and 36,000 sinews (for use in the construction of composite bows),

A German armourer and his apprentice, in a woodcut illustration in *Spiegel des menschlichen Lebens* by Rodericus Zamoriensis, Augsburg 1479. (Staatsbibliothek Preussischer Kulturbesitz)

'Young men killing each other' –
a German manuscript, probably
from Trier, dated *c.*1200.
(*Jungfrauenspiegel*, Kestner-
Museum, Hannover)

plus also birch bark to cover 1,200 crossbows, at the *Schnitzhaus* (carving house) of Marienburg, along with supplies of fishglue and glue made by rendering down the neck hides of cattle.

Information concerning the Teutonic Knights' armour is less detailed, though it seems that there was more experimentation in armour within Germany and Italy than in France or England during the later 13th and 14th centuries. Body armour developed remarkably during the 14th century, an early coat-of-plates found at Küssnach in Switzerland consisting of two sets of plates, front and back, joined over the shoulders and probably laced at the sides. A rudimentary breastplate for the upper chest appeared around 1340 as part of a coat-of-plates, but did not extend below the diaphragm before 1360. Experimentation also concerned materials until the adoption of 'white', that is usually steel, armour in the later 14th century. This experimentation may have reflected problems not only with weight and cost but also with the availability of skilled craftsmen to shape substantial pieces of iron, only the helmet-makers previously doing this. It has also been suggested by Sir James Mann (a former Master of the Armouries at the Tower of London) that the coming together of German and Italian styles of armour resulted in the 'round and fluted armours of the Maximilian fashion at the end of his reign' (Emperor Maximilian I, 1459–1519), such Maximilian armour clearly being used by the Teutonic Knights.

A: Teutonic Knights defend settlers in Cumania, early 13th century

A

B: Arms and Armour of the Teutonic Knights, 13th century, and heraldry associated with the Teutonic Order

C: Teutonic Knights negotiate the surrender of their convent in Acre, 1291

c

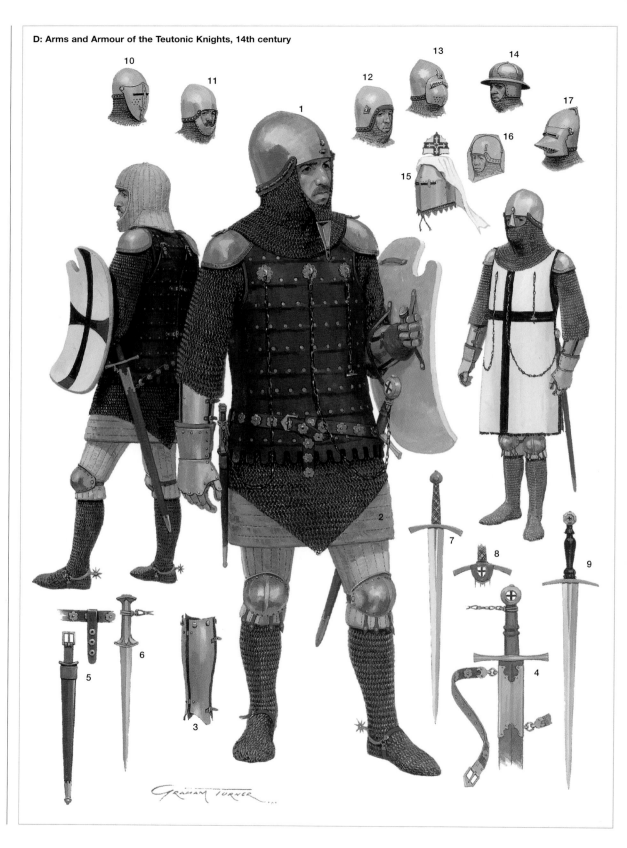

D

F

G: Arms and armour of the Teutonic Knights, second half of the 15th century

G

In its early years, the Order acquired military equipment from a remarkable variety of sources. One Italian crusader named Barzella Merxadrus of Bologna, who died during the Fifth Crusade, stated in his will that: 'To the Hospital of the Germans where he wished to be buried, he left all his arms and armour, and his panceriam with one long sleeve and coif.' There may have been greater efforts at uniformity during the 14th century and under *Hochmeister* Luther von Braunschweig when, for example, the brethren were instructed to have military equipment 'according to the customs of the country', which would have meant mail hauberks and coats-of-plates.

The *Tresslerbuch* ('Treasurer's Book'; financial accounts) of the castle at Marienburg provides detailed information about the Order's military equipment between the years 1399 and 1409. The armour included mail and plate, some specifically of iron, some of steel, some 'white', some 'coloured'. Helmets were again of the expected types, including those with 'dogface' visors. Interestingly, there were more helmets than armours. Other sources shed light on other items. For example, in the

The front of the iron elements of a German coat-of-plates found in the castle of Küssnach, 1340–60. (Gessler Number 1, Swiss National Museum, inv. LM-13367, Zurich)

14th century Teutonic Knights' cavalry adopted a large rectangular shield against Lithuanian javelins and arrows. An almost rectangular shield had been used by Prussians and Lithuanians since at least the early 14th century, the characteristic protruding 'keel' down the front first appearing around 1360.

The close-combat weapons used by the Teutonic Knights were identical to those in Germany, though it would be interesting to know whether lower-status *Halb-brüder* sergeants or local auxiliaries made use of captured Lithuanian swords, several surviving examples of which have highly distinctive forms of hilt. Once the crossbow became widespread in the Teutonic Knights' state, two major forms emerged: the *Steigreifarmbrust* (stirrup bow) and the *Ruckarmbrust* (back crossbow) – by 1390 the stirrup type was much more common. These were the same as those seen elsewhere in Europe, the former being spanned by placing a

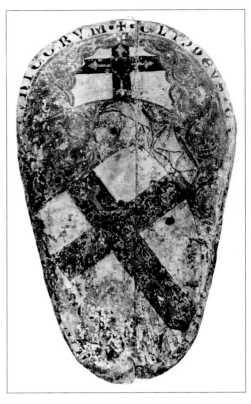

ABOVE **The shield of Conrad II of Thüringia and Hessen,** *Hochmeister* **of the Teutonic Knights 1239–40, with a smaller escutcheon of the Order of Teutonic Knights added at a later date. (Elisabethkirche, Marburg)**

ABOVE RIGHT **Parade shield with the full coat of arms of the** *Hochmeister* **of the Teutonic Knights, made for Carl Beffart von Trier in the early 14th century. (Museum Ferdinandeum, Innsbruck)**

foot into the stirrup and the latter almost certainly by placing both feet on either side of the stock. Both could incorporate simple wooden or composite bowstaves. In European crossbows with composite bows, the 'horn' element was usually baleen whalebone, except in Teutonic Knights' territory where the use of goat or ox horn might indicate eastern influence.

The spanning systems were similar to those used elsewhere, the earliest form of spanning aid being an iron hook or pair of hooks on a broad hip-belt. The so-called 'goatsfoot' spanning lever came into use in Germany during the 14th century, whereas the 'strap and roller' type of geared belt-hook spanning device became popular from the early 15th century onwards. The early 15th century similarly saw the emergence of several forms of windlass and cranequin spanning devices; however the cranequin was perhaps too expensive and complex for extensive use under wartime conditions.

Financial accounts not only distinguished between new and old, large and small crossbows, but also between *gemeine* (ordinary), *knüttel* (perhaps composite), *diener* (servants), *gesellen* (for members of the Order) and *schützen* (target) types. Meanwhile, *Holmische Armbrüste*, imported from Stockholm, were highly prized amongst the Teutonic Knights in the late 14th century. Larger crossbows for use in siege warfare were similarly used in the Teutonic Knights' territories, as they were in northern Germany. Amongst the Teutonic Knights the largest 14th-century windlass or rampart crossbow was often called a *Bankarmbrost* after the 'bank' or bench on which it was placed for spanning or shooting. However, these largest types soon fell out of favour.

It was, of course, vital for garrisons to have sufficient crossbow bolts to withstand a long siege, these being almost as important as food and water. In 1420, for example, there were 63 chests of bolts in the castle of Schochau's 'bolt room'. Schochau also had nine sheaves of 'arrows for back-crossbows and also for arquebuses', which suggests that heavy arrows were still being shot from hand-held guns. In addition there were 250 freshly shafted bolts, six sheaves of unshafted *Bromsar* or *Bremsen* ('gadflies' or 'horseflies' – probably short arrows or bolts for crossbows), 50 sheaves of feathered bolt shafts, one-and-a-half sheaves of fire arrows, and eight sheaves of arrows put aside 'for Hammerstein', a town on the east bank of the Rhine in western Germany. The Teutonic Knights also adopted firearms with enthusiasm, some cannon and smaller guns apparently being manufactured within their territory, though most were imported from Germany.

During their conquest of Prussia, the Teutonic Knights came across the small, indigenous horse known as a *Sweik* or *Schweike*, which was closely related to the *Tarpan* wild horse of eastern Europe. The *Sweik* was used by the native Prussians and Lithuanians as a war horse but, although the Teutonic Knights bred these animals, they were ridden by couriers and local auxiliaries as well as being used in baggage trains, for pulling wagons and in farm work. They also had the advantage of being cheap as well as tough enough to cope with the climate, the cost of even an ordinary warhorse normally being three or four times that of a *Sweik* by the year 1400.

Guards at the Holy Sepulchre, **an Alsacian carved stone altar showing German infantry of the late 15th or early 16th century. (*In situ* Church of SS Peter and Paul, Obernai; author's photograph)**

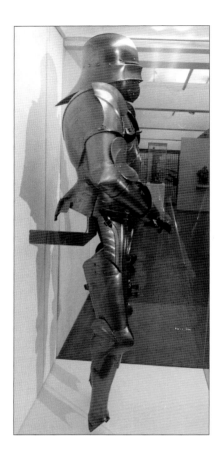

RIGHT **Armour in German 'Gothic' style made by the Missaglia workshop in Milan, probably for export to Germany, in the second half of the 15th century. (Städt. Museum, Schwäbisch. Gmünd, Württemberg; photograph U. Koch)**

FAR RIGHT **German fluted armour for the field c.1525. (Collection of The Duke of Brunswick)**

TRAINING AND CAMPAIGNING

Martial skills

Although little specific information is available concerning military training amongst the Teutonic Knights, it was probably comparable to that in other military orders, and would have reflected the high development of martial skills within the German Empire. In late 12th- and early 13th-century Austria, for example, the *Nibelungenlied* epic referred to jousting in the castle yard as a form of training. Young warriors also demonstrated their strength by 'putting the weight or throwing the javelin', while displays of 'fencing under the shield' were organized to impress visitors.

The oldest surviving Western European book on sword fighting was written in Germany, in Latin, around 1300, but as it largely concerned fencing with sword and buckler it may have been intended for civilians rather than the knightly class from whom the Teutonic Order largely recruited. Nevertheless, it was evidence of a highly developed system and perhaps long established traditions, though not necessarily in Germany itself. This form of book was also a forerunner of the characteristic later medieval German *Fechtbuch* (fighting book). It seems that by the mid-14th century the most highly developed 'schools' of swordplay in Western Europe were in Germany and Italy, but quite why this should be remains a mystery and may merely reflect the survival of German and Italian rather than other texts. One specific piece of information does refer to the Teutonic Knights' Baltic state. In 1354 the *Hochmeister* ordered that 'a tree with a bird' be set up in every city as a crossbow training target; the wooden bird was as big as a hen with outstretched wings and painted various colours, which is why it was called a *popinjay* or 'parrot'.

Campaign conditions

The Teutonic Knights' campaigns in the Middle East and even Hungary were essentially the same as those conducted by other Western European military forces. In the Baltic region, however, things tended to be different because of the climate, terrain and the opponents they faced. Here the winters obliged 'northern crusaders' to learn new strategies and tactics. Prussian, Livonian and Lithuanian winters could be so fierce that infantry died on the march, and snow was so deep that cavalry rode single file through trenches where the snow had been cut away. At other times the snow was too thick to travel through at all. Henry of Livonia wrote of winter in this region: 'snow covered the land and ice covered the waves … the waves were as hard as stone.' Yet a mild winter could be worse, with frozen rivers not strong enough to support horses or mud making tracks impassable. Mud plagued the spring thaw, when it was virtually impossible to move on the muddy land or in rivers swollen with meltwater.

Summer floods or sudden winter thaws could trap armies without hope of relief, and it was thought prudent to divide armies into several groups so that not all would get trapped or delayed. Weather forecasting was non-existent in the modern sense, and so prospective crusader volunteers could not know if there would be a campaign next year or not. In 1394, Duke Philip of Burgundy wrote to the *Hochmeister* asking if there would be such a *reysa* or raiding campaign. Conrad von Jungingen replied that he could not predict, 'because it is impossible to provide a truthful forecast of future contingencies, especially since on our expeditions we are obliged to go across great waters and vast solitudes by dangerous ways …'

Severe winter caused great losses of horses. Nor was the often-waterlogged ground good pasture for horses, producing sour, tough grass. Sodden, spongy hooves broke under heavy burdens, skin saturated in raw muddy conditions produced rain scald and mud fever. Technology could help, with 'unhardened' horseshoes being used in summer whereas 'hardened' versions were necessary in winter. A reliable supply of suitable horseshoes was vital and at one point there were over 13,000 in the forge of the castle at Balga alone. Losses of horses were entered into the Order's *Tresslerbuch* which, for example, listed how 24 German nobles from Kulmerland lost 50 destriers (war-horses), trotters and other horses during one campaign in western Lithuania in the summer of 1402. This was recorded because the Teutonic Knights had to replace the animals, as the campaign went beyond the boundaries of normal feudal service.

The strategic heritage of the Teutonic Knights was that of high-medieval Western Europe – its three main elements were armoured cavalry, crossbowmen and those who built castles. What differed was the degree of ruthlessness, the forced conversion and occasional extermination of those who resisted. In the Baltic, the military orders were also much more advanced than their foes in fortification and siege warfare, though their enemies remained numerically far superior. Castles, therefore, served as secure bases from which to campaign and into which to retreat. If their provisions lasted, the major castles usually held out against attacks and it was usually only small forts that fell.

The Teutonic Knights' conquest of Prussia consisted of gradually pushing the frontier forward, with newly won tracts of land being protected by fortresses and cultivated by the remaining local population plus new settlers. The Knights' campaigns against the Lithuanians largely relied upon traditional raid-and-devastate tactics, which had been typical of the Baltic region before the crusaders arrived. Even after gaining almost complete control of the Baltic coast in 1260, the Teutonic Knights and their supporters remained few and vulnerable. Prussian uprisings were so serious that on at least one occasion only a massive crusading effort from Western Europe saved the Order. The *Hochmeisters* were also fortunate in being allowed to use such reinforcements as they thought best, without the division of command that plagued the crusades in the Middle East.

Then there were the Mongols who raided deep into Prussia and inflicted heavy losses in 1259. Little is known about the relatively minor clashes between Teutonic Knights and Mongols in the Baltic region in the 1260s, but the Papacy put great effort into the development of a sophisticated system of communications in Eastern Europe to keep an eye on the Mongol threat. After this threat faded, the Teutonic Knights focused on their primary foe, the Grand Duchy of Lithuania. There were campaigns almost every year from 1283 until 1406, long after the Lithuanians had converted to Christianity. Despite huge expenditure of money and labour, and atrocities and widespread devastation, neither side was strong enough to destroy the other's military or economic resources.

Most of the fighting was within an area of deciduous forest, heath and marsh. With their dense undergrowth, the Baltic forests were unlike the generally open coniferous forests farther north. At its centre were the upper Niemen, Vilya and Dvina rivers, where the Lithuanians and their newly conquered Russian subjects cleared enough land to support a large population, while still leaving a belt of uncleared forest over 150km (93 miles) wide between themselves and the Teutonic Knights in Prussia and Livonia. It was not, in fact, the trees that formed the main barrier – it was the dense undergrowth, marshes and numerous waterways that really obstructed the movement of forces.

Most warfare consisted of raiding by relatively small forces, the crusaders learning as early as 1211 to use frozen rivers as 'winter roads'. In fact the crusaders and military orders soon did more winter raiding than the pagans. Summer raiding was less frequent, but was usually on a larger scale and, during the early decades, was often by sea. In all seasons, the most reliable method of reaching the enemy was for a raiding party to be led by an experienced woodsman or *Leitzlute* (guide). Moderately sized forces could erect earth and timber forts within a few weeks, though these were again more characteristic of summer campaigns. Meanwhile, the Prussians and Lithuanians became militarily more sophisticated. By the first half of the 14th century, for example, the Lithuanians and Teutonic Knights had a good understanding of each other's difficulties and weaknesses. As a result, the Lithuanians raided in mid-September each year, when the Teutonic Knights would be assembling in 'General Chapter' and some of their garrisons were thus weakened.

The most dreaded territory was the *Grauden*, north-east of Königsberg, the sparsely populated ancestral home of the Zhemaitui or Samogitians. From the 13th to 15th centuries it effectively separated the

Teutonic Knights' territories in Prussia and Livonia while also forming a buffer between the Knights' garrisons and the Lithuanian heartland. The frontier itself consisted of a strip of land of varying width between the recognized outposts or fortifications of each side. The *Littauischen Wegeberiche* (Livonian Roads Book), written between 1384 and 1402, described the routes between Prussia and Lithuania. To take just one example, if a raiding force reached Betygala near the upper Dubysa River (a tributary of the Niemen flowing from Samogitia) and wanted to go to Vandziogala north of Kaunas, a distance of a mere 34km (21 miles) in a straight line, it would face exceptionally tough going. First the track crossed scrubland, then it went through a forest where men needed to

A 15th-century wall painting of the Teutonic Knights' Grand Masters Ludolf von Konig (1341–45) and Heinrich von Plauen (1410–13). (*In situ* cathedral, Kwidzyn; photograph Stephen Turnbull)

clear their own way, then over another heath and through another wood 'the length of a crossbow shot and there you have to clear your way also'. Next came another heath and another wood that entailed trail-cutting for 5km (3 miles), and even this only took you to the edge of true *Wiltnisse* (wilderness). A route found by a Prussian scout was described in a letter to the Teutonic Knights' marshal that was later inserted into the *Littauischen Wegeberiche*:

> Dear Lord Marshal, Take notice in your wisdom that by God's grave, Gedutte [the name of the scout] and his company have got back in safety and have completed everything you sent us to carry out and have marked the way so far as four and a half miles this side of the Niemen, along a route that crosses the Niemen and leads straight into the country.

The company had travelled nearly 115km (71½ miles) as the crow flies, in nine stages, each of which was marked by a 'night camp', and they reported the presence of many people and houses 'in the waste', but nothing like a proper road suitable for armies or merchants.

Armies frequently got lost or failed to find their enemy; 20km (12½ miles) was considered a good day's journey, which could be considerably less. Only the rivers Niemen and Dvina offered a secure passage for bulk transport, but even these presented problems, the upper Dvina being fast flowing in places and channelled between steep banks, while the tributaries flowing out of Lithuania were narrow and shallow. The Niemen was much more placid, but was also so winding that a ship's crew could spend a whole day going round a curve and still be within walking distance of their previous night's camp.

'Siege scene' in *Rudolf von Ems Weltchronik*. (Zentralbib. Zurich, Ms. Rh. 16, f. 197r)

The earliest years of the Baltic crusades had an important naval dimension, with the maritime campaigns often following existing trade routes. As the coasts and islands came under Christian control, however, the naval aspect of the Baltic crusades became a matter of moving men and supplies and the Teutonic Knights began to make use of larger ships early in the 13th century. The most significant were large *cogs*, which gave the Order a clear technological advantage, some being able to carry more than ten times the load of the old *byrthing* or *keel*. The *cog* also had several advantages as a fighting ship, being notably higher in the water than the old Viking-style longships.

Siege warfare

Although the Teutonic Knights occasionally attacked the fortifications of their pagan and subsequently fellow-Christian foes, it was defensive siege warfare that featured more prominently in their thinking. Even as late as the mid-13th century, there were probably no more than five stone or brick fortifications in Teutonic Knights Prussia, and around ten in Livonia, yet these enabled small Christian garrisons to survive against far more numerous foes. German and Scandinavian naval domination also meant that the crusaders had plenty of expertise in the handling of ropes and heavy baulks of timber, such skills being shared by sailors and siege engineers.

Examples of successful siege campaigns by the Teutonic Knights include the seizure of Danzig and Pomerania in 1309. One target was the traditional earth-and-timber fortress of Swiecie, which was also protected by water on three sides. Here the Teutonic Knights used four stone-throwing machines, probably counterweight trebuchets, plus wooden siege towers, to which the defenders could only reply with large and small crossbows mounted on, or operated from, their ramparts. The slaughter of defeated garrisons was not uncommon, at least until King John of Bohemia insisted on sparing the 6,000 Samogitians who surrendered at Medewage in 1329. At other times the slaughter was not carried out by the victors but by the vanquished, as in 1336 when the Lithuanian defenders of Pilene killed their own wives, children and then each other rather than surrender.

The Order began to use firearms during the second half of the 14th century, initially in siege operations, but more traditional skills continued to be needed. During the final Polish siege of Marienburg in 1459–60, the Teutonic Knights tried to strengthen the garrison by sending supply boats upriver. These were slowed down by ice in a river that was only just thawing and shortly before they arrived they were ambushed by enemy troops, who tipped the cargoes into the river before making off. Only a few barrels of pork fat, munitions, and 24 handguns were retrieved by the garrison. In their desperation, the garrison eventually expelled the women, children and elderly from Marienburg because there were too many mouths to feed, but the besiegers forced them back inside again.

'Siege of a fortress by Duke Philip the Good of Burgundy', mid-15th-century carved reliefs. (*In situ* Stadhuis, Leuven; author's photograph)

THE EXPERIENCE OF BATTLE

In open combat, according to Henry of Livonia, the Germans' heavier armour for men and horses gave them a physical and psychological advantage over the indigenous peoples. The crusaders' crossbows were even more significant, this new weapon having been used by the Danes against pagan Slav Wends around 1170. Though the Germans were slower to adopt the crossbow than some other Western European peoples, their settlers in the Baltic were clearly soon doing so. On the other hand, the local peoples and Russians rapidly copied the Western European crusaders' crossbows and siege machines; this process of technology transfer was made easier by the crusaders' employment of indigenous troops as auxiliaries.

Henry of Livonia knew about warfare between crusaders and Baltic pagans either at first hand or from contact with those who had taken part, and his description of a battle in 1207 is particularly revealing:

> The Lithuanians flew around on their speedy horses. As was their custom they rode about here and there, sometimes fleeing, sometimes pursuing, threw their lances and javelins and wounded many. The Germans, however, grouping themselves together into a single wedge and protecting the army from the rear, permitted the Semgalls [local auxiliaries] to go ahead.

This time the auxiliaries fled and the Christians were defeated.

Poor visibility in dense woodland as well as boggy terrain frequently hindered fully armoured Teutonic Knights' cavalry tactics in the Baltic region, while the heightened threat of ambush probably meant that men wore armour on the march to a greater extent than was normal. In battle, caltrops proved effective against enemy horsemen, but sometimes caused problems by injuring friendly cavalry. Other evidence suggests that local converts tended to be placed on the flanks of a Teutonic Knights' battle array, with the élite of German knights in the centre.

A clash that sheds considerable light on the tactics of the Teutonic Knights, and those of their Lithuanian foes, occurred during a Lithuanian raid against the island of Ösel early in 1270. The raiders had crossed the frozen Gulf of Riga to reach the island. They were, however, intercepted by the army of the bishop of Leal and a force of Teutonic Knights. So the Lithuanians dismounted and lashed their sledges together as a field

Knights in combat in a replica of a German wall painting, 1227. (Castle Museum, Wartburg; author's photograph)

fortification on the sea ice. The Teutonic Knights charged, but their main force attacked too early, was separated from its colleagues and became entangled amongst the sledges. Many horses were cut down before the bishop's troops on the left and the Danes in the centre scattered many of the Lithuanians then pursued the fugitives. Unfortunately for the crusaders, much of the Lithuanian force remained in place and it took time for the Christian cavalry to reassemble. Several further charges then drove the pagans away from the Christian infantry, who were in danger of being overrun. As night fell, the Lithuanians still held the 'field', though the crusader army was still intact. The raiders then stripped the dead and made their way home with substantial booty, this success encouraging other Lithuanian tribes to join in the war. To quote from the Livonian Rhymed Chronicle:

Knights fighting with swords on a carved capital from the Teutonic Knights' castle at Kwidzin, early 14th century. (Castle Museum, inv. MZM/DA/5, Malbork; photo Lech Okonski)

One could see a disorderly tumult of the two armies,
Christian and heathen.
The battle was hard fought,
And the blood flowed onto the ice from either side.
It was a fight in which many
Noble men were struck down.
Slain in defeat was good Master Otto,
And fifty-two good brothers.
They spilled their blood for God.
Also many outstanding chivalrous warriors
On both sides fell.
Part of the natives [auxiliaries] fell.
May God save their souls.

Within an army the proportions of Teutonic brethren, both knights and sergeants, to other troops including local auxiliaries clearly varied. Even in the Kulm area, which had been under the Teutonic Knights' control almost from the start of their Baltic campaigns, only an estimated 7.5 per cent of their forces were heavily armoured horsemen. Elsewhere the proportion was even lower.

One of the most famous scenes in Eisenstein's film *Alexander Nezsky* shows a portable organ being played during an open-air religious service before the battle of Lake Peipus. The chronicler Henry of Livonia referred to such instruments and may himself have been the priest who, during a pagan siege of the crusader castle at Beverin, stood on the ramparts to 'pray' on a musical instrument. There was also a bell in the city of Riga that was only rung in time of war. During the early 13th century, the Germans and other crusaders raised their morale before battle with drums, pipes and other musical instruments. The indigenous Livs and Letts did so by

Early 16th-century wall painting of the Teutonic Knights in combat. Their foes are shown as turbanned Muslims. (Historical Museum, Torun; photograph Stephen Turnbull)

clashing their swords and shields together, while the Livonians' auxiliary infantry marched ahead of the knights in an orderly fashion, singing and beating on drums. The Russians were described as using 'drums and pipes' to reassemble their army after crossing a river in Estonia.

On campaign, the brethren and servants of the Teutonic Order were subject to strict discipline, the *Marschall* being permitted to use his 'baton' upon the brethren in battle and his 'rod' in camp. The distinction between these two implements is, however, less clear. On the march, the tent of the *Meister* or of the *Marschall* was used as a field chapel where a full cycle of 'hours', religious services and observances, was performed within earshot of the guards. Other strict regulations dealt with parades, route marches, pitching camp, guard duty and conduct on the field of battle, all to be carried out in silence.

During and immediately after battle it was normal to slaughter the enemy wounded and to massacre fleeing foes, especially if the latter were pagans or schismatic. Such behaviour was not regarded as cruel and it has been suggested that the carnage illustrated in several 'militarized Bibles' from the period of the crusades is closer to the reality of warfare than the sanitized injuries pictured in chivalric texts such as *chansons de geste* (Old French for 'songs of heroic deeds'). It is also worth noting that studies of skeletons from medieval battle sites say virtually nothing about injuries to soft tissue and vital organs.

Apart from death or injury, there was always the possibility of capture, and it is clear that human beings were the most important form of booty for both sides in warfare between Teutonic Knights and

Lithuanians. Hundreds of thousands of people were probably abducted in this manner. Those captured by the pagans could expect permanent slavery, but a more varied fate may have awaited those captured by the Christians. Even here, however, captives might be slaughtered if they became a burden in difficult circumstances. The majority of those who survived are likely to have been used as slave labour in the cities, castles or agricultural villages of Teutonic Knights' territory. A brutally frank description of what were, in reality, slaving raids, came from the pen of the Austrian poet-herald Peter Suchenwirt who witnessed the Baltic campaign of Duke Albert III of Austria in 1337:

> Women and children were taken captive;
> What a jolly medley could be seen.
> Many a woman could be seen,
> Two children tied to her body,
> One behind and one in front. On a horse without spurs,
> Barefoot they had ridden here,
> The heathen were made to suffer,
> Many were captured and in every case,
> Were their hands tied together,
> They were led off, all tied up,
> Just like hunting dogs.

If an auxiliary in the service of the Teutonic Knights captured a Lithuanian warrior above a certain 'rank', he was obliged to sell their captive to the Order for a fixed sum. One such tariff, recorded in the indenture made with the lords of Strammel and Manteuffel in 1390, specified 500 Prussian Marks for a king, 100 for a duke and 50 for a count. These were not large sums bearing in mind that freelance auxiliary leaders could be paid 5,400 Prussian Marks for a year's service with their retinues. So perhaps the Order made a substantial profit on the resale or ransoming of high-status captives.

Knights jousting, on a carved capital from the Teutonic Knights' castle at Kwidzin, early 14th century. (Castle Museum, inv. MZM/DA/5, Malbork; photograph Lech Okonski)

COLLECTIONS AND SIGNIFICANT HISTORICAL LOCATIONS

Very few surviving pieces of military equipment can definitely be associated with the Teutonic Knights. They do, however, include fragments found by archaeologists at Montfort in the Galilee region of northern Israel. Although this fortress was the headquarters of the Order for much of the 13th century, several of the military objects recovered there could be Islamic in origin, since Montfort was garrisoned by Mamluk troops after the Teutonic Knights were expelled. Such fragments include pieces of arrows with tanged and socketed arrowheads, crossbow boltheads, a blade and butt from a spear or javelin, some scales from an armour that is more likely Mamluk, and a piece of perforated iron that some have optimistically described as part of a 13th-century great helm. Two oversized metal 'thimbles' from Montfort were probably archer's finger guards, as used when shooting a clay pellet. Both Christians and Muslims hunted with such pellets in the Middle East. The objects from Montfort are currently divided between the Israel Antiquities Department and the Metropolitan Museum of Art in New York.

No arms or armour from 13th- and 14th-century Europe have been firmly linked with the Teutonic Knights. However, some armours from close to the Teutonic Knights' Baltic state were preserved in the collection of the Duke of Brunswick and Lüneburg. Most are typical German fluted armour of the very early 16th century and are currently in private hands. An exceptionally rare example of a piece of armour that can be directly linked with the Teutonic Knights is a breastplate engraved with the arms of the *Hochmeister*. Again dating from the early 16th century, it may have been made for Margrave Albrecht von Hohenzollern, the last *Hochmeister* in Prussia, and is currently in the Historisches Museum of Dresden.

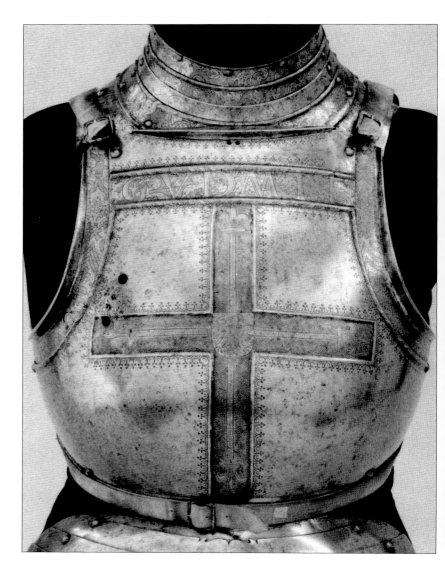

An early 16th-century breastplate with the engraved arms of the *Hochmeister*, perhaps made for Albrecht von Hohenzollern, the last *Hochmeister* in Prussia. (Historisches Museum, Dresden)

The most distinctive surviving castle of the Teutonic Knights in the Middle East is Montfort. The structures that have been excavated include the castle plus a guest hall and mill complex lower down the hill. Much less survives of the other castles held by the Teutonic Knights in Palestine. These include Rahab, whose minimal remains are now part of the Israeli settlement of Mezad Rahav, which is on the tense border with Lebanon. Haruniye, north of Antioch in Turkey, is certainly worth visiting, though it is difficult to reach and is more significant as an example of early Islamic rather than crusader military architecture. Similarly, only a small part of nearby Amouda dates from the Teutonic Knights' occupation.

Main gate of Haruniye castle north of Antioch, probably strengthened after the Teutonic Knights took over in the 13th century. (Author's photograph)

The Teutonic Knights' castles, urban fortifications and citadels in northern Poland, Lithuania, Latvia, Estonia and the Russian enclave of Kaliningrad are amongst the most remarkable in Europe. They are varied, dramatic, and in some cases extensively restored. Sadly, the citadel of Königsberg was entirely demolished in 1950s and 1960s in Soviet acts of vengeance. Even so, a greater number of battered examples of Teutonic Knights' architecture survive in Kaliningrad than is generally realized. Little has been published about other fortifications within the Russian enclave, but some structures survive. The newly reorganized Museum of History and Art in Kaliningrad is making a courageous effort to emerge from the Soviet era with a display covering the entire history and culture of the enclave. There is also a small museum on the site of the battlefield of Tannenberg in Poland.

The military branches of the Teutonic Knights were dissolved in Austria in 1923, though the Order continues to work as a charitable organization of Catholic priests and sisters. The archives of the Teutonic Order similarly survive as the *Zentralarchiv des Deutschen Ordens* (DOZA), housed at Singerstrasse 7, 1010, Vienna, Austria. It is open from Monday to Friday, 9.30am to 12.30pm by appointment, and at the time of writing those wishing to consult this archive should contact Father Dr Bernhard Demel OT.

BIBLIOGRAPHY

Arnold, U., *Die Stadt in Preussen* (Luneburg, 1983)

Arnold, U. (ed.), *Zur Wirtschaftensentwicklung des Deutschen Ordens in Mittelalter* (Marburg, 1988)

Arnold, U. (ed.), *800 Jahre Deutscher Orden* (Munich, 1990)

Benninghoven, F. (ed.), *Unter Kreuz und Adler: der Deutsche Orden im Mittelalter* (Mainz, 1990)

Bogdan, H., *Les chevaliers teutoniques* (Paris, 1995)

Bookman, H., *Der Deutsche Orden* (Berlin, 1981)

Brundage, J., 'The Thirteenth Century Livonian Crusades: Henricus de Lettis and the First Legative Mission of Bishop William of Modena', *Jahrbücher für Geschichte Osteuropas*, n.s. 20 (1972) 1–9

Burleigh, M., *Prussian Society and the German Order: An Aristocratic Corporation in Crisis c.1410–1460* (Cambridge, 1984)

Chodynski, A. R., 'The Significance of the Lost Painting of the Siege of Malbork in 1460 from Dwór Artusa', in W. Swietoslawski (ed.), *Warfare in the Middle Ages: Acta Archaeologica Lodziensia*, 47 (Lodz 2001) 83–99

Czacharowski, A. (ed.), *Etudes sur l'histoire de l'Ordre teutoniques et de son Etat (Ordines Militaires 2)* (Torun, 1984)

Dean, B., 'A Crusader Fortress in Palestine (Montfort)', *Bulletin of the Metropolitan Museum of Art*, 22/2 (1927) 91–97

Demel, B., 'Hospitality and Chivalry in the Teutonic Order', in M. Barber (ed.), *The Military Orders: Fighting for the Faith and Caring for the Sick* (Aldershot, 1994) 278–82

Demel, B., 'Welfare and Warfare in the Teutonic Order: A Survey', in H. Nicholson (ed.), *The Military Orders, vol. 2: Welfare and Warfare* (Aldershot, 1998) 61–74

Dollinger, P., 'Aspects de la noblesse allemande, XIe-XIIIe siecles", in P. Contamine (ed.), *La Noblesse au Moyen Age* (Paris, 1976) 133–52

Ehlers, A., 'The Crusade of the Teutonic Knights against Lithuania reconsidered', in A. V. Murray (ed.), *Crusade and Conversion on the Baltic Frontier 1150–1500* (Aldershot, 2001) 21–44

Ekdahl, S., 'The Treatment of Prisoners of War during the Fighting between the Teutonic Order and Lithuania', in M. Barber (ed.), *The Military Orders: Fighting for the Faith and Caring for the Sick* (Aldershot, 1994) 263–69

Ekdahl, S., 'Horses and Crossbows: Two Important Warfare Advantages of the Teutonic Order in Prussia', in H. Nicholson (ed.), *The Military Orders, vol. 2: Welfare and Warfare* (Aldershot, 1998) 119–52

Ekdahl, S., 'The Strategic Organization of the Commanderies of the Teutonic Order in Prussia and Livonia', in A. Luttrell & L. Pressouyre (eds), *La Commanderie, institution des ordres militaires dans l'Occident médiévales* (Paris, 2002) 219–42

Engel, B., 'Nachrichten über Waffen aus dem Tresslerbuche des Deutschen Ordens', *Zeitschrift für Historische Waffenkunde*, 1 (Dresden, 1897–99)

Favreau-Lilie, M-L., 'The Teutonic Knights in Acre after the fall of Montfort (1271): Some Reflections', in B. Z. Kedar et al. (eds), *Outremer: Studies in the History of the Crusading Kingdom of Jerusalem* (Jerusalem, 1982) 272–84

Favreau-Lilie, M-L., 'Alle origine dell'Ordine Teutonico: continuita a nuova fondazione dell'Ospedale gerosolimitano degle Alemanni?' in Coli, E. (ed.), *Militia Sacra, Gli ordini militari tra Europa e Terrasanta* (Perugia, 1994) 29–47

Gaier, C., 'Quelques particularites de l'armement des Chevaliers Teutoniques dans le baillage Germani Inferieure aux XIVe et XVe siecles', in A. Nadolski (ed.), *Fasciculi Archaeologiae Historicae* (Wroclaw, 1986)

Glassl, H., 'Der Deutsche Orden im Burgenland und in Kumanien (1211–1225)', *Ungarn Jahrbüch*, 3 (1971) 23–49

Górski, K., 'The Teutonic Order in Prussia', *Medievalia et Humanistica*, 17 (1966) 20–37

Jensen, C. S., K. V. Jensen & J. H. Lind, 'Communicating Crusades and Crusading Communications in the Baltic Region', *Scandinavian Economic History Review*, 49 (2001) 5–25

Kajzer, L., 'Remarks on the Architecture of the Teutonic Order's Castles in Prussia', in Z. Hunyadi (ed.), *The Crusades and the Military Orders* (Budapest, 2001)

Kulakov, V. I., *Prussia Antiqua vol. 1: Istoriya Prussii do 1283 goda* (Moscow, 2003)

Laszlovszky, J., & Z. Soos, 'Historical Monuments of the Teutonic Order in Transylvania', in Z. Hunyadi (ed.), *The Crusades and the Military Orders: Expanding the Frontiers of Medieval Latin Christianity* (Budapest, 2001) 317–36

Markov, D. D. De, 'The Battle of Tannenberg (Grunwald) in 1410', in *From Crecy to Mohacs; Warfare in the Late Middle Ages* (London, 1997) 300–05

Militzer, K., 'The Recruitment of Brethren for the Teutonic Order in Livonia 1237–1562', in M. Barber (ed.), *The Military Orders: Fighting for the Faith and Caring for the Sick* (Aldershot, 1994) 270–77

Militzer, K., 'Der Wein des Meisters. Die Weinversorgung des Hochmeisters des Deutschen Ordens in Preussen', in O. Pelc & G. Pickhan (eds), *Zwischen Lübeck und Novgorod. Wirtschaft, Politik und Kultur im Ostseeraum vom frühen Mittelalter bis ins. 20 Jahrhundert* (Lüneburg, 1996) 143–55

Militzer, K., 'The Role of Hospitals in the Teutonic Order', in H. Nicholson (ed.), *The Military Orders, vol. 2: Welfare and Warfare* (Aldershot, 1998) 51–60

Militzer, K., 'From the Holy Land to Prussia: the Teutonic Knights between Emperors and Popes and their Policies until 1309', in J. Sarnowsky (ed.), *Mendicants, Military Orders and Regionalism in Medieval Europe* (Aldershot, 1999) 71–81

Militzer, K., *Von Akkon zur Marienburg, Verfassung, Verwaltung und Sozialstruktur des Deutschen Ordens 1190–1309: Quellen und Studien zur Geschichte des Deutschen Ordens*, 56 (Bad Godesberg, 1999)

Nicholson, H., *Templars, Hospitallers and Teutonic Knights: Images of the Military Orders 1128–1291* (Leicester, 1993)

Nicholson, H., *Love, War and the Grail: the Templars, Hospitallers and Teutonic Knights in Medieval Epic and Romance c.1150–1500* (Leiden, 2000)

Nickel, H., 'Some Heraldic Fragments Found at Castle Montfort/Starkenberg in 1926 and the Arms of the Grand Master of the Teutonic Knights', *Metropolitan Museum Journal*, 24 (1989) 35–46

Nowakowski, A., *Arms and Armour of the Medieval Teutonic Order's State of Prussia* (in Polish version with English summary) (Lodz, 1980)

Olins, P. Z., *The Teutonic Knights in Latvia* (Riga, 1928)

Perlbach, M. (ed.), *Die Statuten des Deutschen Ordens* (Halle, 1890)

Powell, J. M., 'Frederick II, the Hohenstaufen, and the Teutonic Order in the Kingdom of Sicily', in M. Barber (ed.), *Military Orders: Fighting for the Faith and Caring for the Sick* (Aldershot, 1994) 236–44

Probable sugarcane press in the Teutonic Knights' castle of Montfort in northern Palestine. (Photograph Rabia Khamissy)

A latrine chute in the Teutonic Knights' castle of Montfort in northern Palestine. (Photograph Rabia Khamissy)

Pringle, R. D., 'A Thirteenth Century Hall at Montfort Castle in Western Galilee', *The Antiquaries Journal*, 66 (1986) 52–81

Probst, C., *Der Deutschen Orden und sein Medizinalwesen in Preussen. Hospital, Firmarie und Arzt bis 1525: Quellen und Studien zur Geschichte des Deutschen Ordens*, 29 (Bad Godesberg, 1969)

Riley-Smith, J. S. C., 'The Templars and the Teutonic Knights in Cilician Armenia', in T. S. R. Boase (ed.), *The Cilician Kingdom of Armenia* (London, 1978) 92–117

Rodriques-Garcia, J. M., 'Alfonso X and the Teutonic Order: an example of the role of the International Military Orders in mid 13th century Castile', in H. Nicholson (ed.), *The Military Orders, vol. 2: Welfare and Warfare* (Aldershot, 1998) 319–28

Sarnowsky, J., 'The Teutonic Order Confronts the Mongols and Turks,' in M. Barber (ed.), *Military Orders: Fighting for the Faith and Caring for the Sick* (Aldershot, 1994) 253–262

Soos, Z., 'Historical Monuments of the Teutonic Order in Transylvania' in Z. Hunyadi (ed.), *The Crusades and the Military Orders* (Budapest, 2001)

Starnawska, M., 'Military Orders and the beginning of Crusades in Prussia, in Z. Hunyadi (ed.), *The Crusades and the Military Orders* (Budapest, 2001)

Tumler, P. M., *Der Deutsche Orden im Werden, Wachsen und Wirken bis 1400* (Vienna, 1954)

Urban, W., 'The Organization and Defence of the Livonian Frontier in the Thirteenth Century', *Speculum*, 48 (1973) 523–32

Urban, W., *The Baltic Crusade* (De Kalb, 1975)

Urban, W., *The Prussian Crusade* (New York, 1980)

Urban, W., 'Roger Bacon and the Teutonic Knights', *Journal of Baltic Studies*, 19 (1989) 331–38

Urban, W., *The Samogitian Crusade* (Chicago, 1989)

Urban, W., 'The Teutonic Order and the Christianization of Lithuania', in anon. (ed.), *La cristianizzazione della Lituania* (Vatican, 1989) 105–35

Urban, W., 'The Teutonic Knights and Baltic Chivalry', *The Historian*, 56 (Spring 1994) 519–30

Urban, W., *Tannenburg and After* (Chicago, 1998)

Urban, W., *The Teutonic Knights, a Military History* (London, 2003)

Van Eickels, K., 'Knightly Hospitallers or Crusading Knight? Decisive factors for the spread of the Teutonic Knights in the Rhineland and the Low Countries, 1216–1300', in H. Hicholson (ed.), *The Military Orders, vol. 2: Welfare and Warfare* (Aldershot, 1998) 75–82

Weiss, D. J., 'Spiritual Life in the Teutonic Order: a Comparison between the Commanderies of Franconia and Prussia', in A. Luttrell & L. Pressouyre (eds), *La Commanderie, institution des ordres militaires dans l'Occident médiéval* (Paris, 2002) 159–73

Wojtecki, D., *Studien zur Personengeschichte des Deutschen Ordens im 13. Jahrhunderts* (Wiesbaden, 1971)

Wunsch, C., *Ost-preussen: Die Kunst im Deutschen Osten* (Berlin, 1960)

Zimmerling, G., *Der Deutsche Ritterorden* (Dusseldorf, 1988)

Zimmermann, H., *Siebenburgen und seine Hospites Theutonici* (Cologne, 1996)

COLOUR PLATE COMMENTARY

A: TEUTONIC KNIGHTS DEFEND SETTLERS IN CUMANIA, EARLY 13TH CENTURY

Having been invited by King Andrew II to stiffen the defence of the south-eastern corner of the vast medieval Kingdom of Hungary, the Teutonic Knights proved so effective that they were soon given authority over additional territory. This appears to have reached across the crest of the wild Carpathian Mountains into what was then called Cumania – now the eastern part of the Rumanian province of Wallachia. Here a remarkably small number of brethren of the Teutonic Order frequently clashed with the largely pagan Turkish Kipchaqs who dominated the region. As part of efforts to consolidate Hungarian control on both sides of the mountains and passes, settlers from Western Europe and other parts of Hungary were encouraged to establish farms, villages, markets and eventually small towns. Many of these settlers came from Germany, mostly it seems from Saxony, which was why the Western settlers were widely referred to as Saxons. In this reconstruction of members of the Teutonic Order defending such a frontier settlement, a Brother Knight (1) has typical early 13th-century German arms and armour, including an iron helmet with a rigid face-mask visor worn over a mail coif beneath the helmet, which is itself an integral part of his mail hauberk. His sleeveless white woolen or linen surcoat has an integral thickly padded or quilted lining on the chest, back and most notably on the shoulders. The black fabric cross sewn on the front of course shows that he is a brother knight. Horse armour, including the quilted style of this brother knight's fallen horse, was popular in Germany and other parts of the Empire. A brother Sergeant of the Teutonic Order (2) has the more limited armour used by nevertheless well-equipped early 13th-century crossbowmen. His separate mail coif is worn over a domed helmet with a substantial nasal protector, which broadens to cover part of his mouth. He is otherwise protected by a grey linen-covered and thickly quilted gambeson soft-armour with long sleeves. The T-shaped 'Tau' or truncated black cross sewn to the front of his gambeson shows that he is a 'half brother' or brother sergeant of the Teutonic Order. In addition to a stirrup-style crossbow he is armed with a normal German sword of this period. The Kipchaq Turkish warrior (3) would appear to be a chieftain or leading warrior, as his arms, armour and horse-harness are of the finest quality available in the wealthy but still largely nomadic Kipchaq Turkish Khanates that extended from what is southern Rumania to north of the Caspian Sea. The settler (4) wears typical 13th-century Western European peasant costume.

B: ARMS AND ARMOUR OF THE TEUTONIC KNIGHTS, 13TH CENTURY, AND HERALDRY ASSOCIATED WITH THE TEUTONIC ORDER

This knight of the 13th century is depicted in typical armour of the period. He wears an unpainted, flat-topped iron great helm (1) made of riveted segments, plus a cross-shaped reinforcement with eye-slits riveted to the front. Three pairs of leather laces through paired holes at the sides of the helmet secure it to the shaped arming cap beneath. A separate mail coif (2) was worn beneath the arming cap; this style with rectangular 'bibs' at the front and back was typical of German examples. The coat-of-plates (3) is covered with white linen cloth – the iron elements of the armour are arranged vertically

and overlap slightly from front to back, waist to neck. They are fastened with iron rivets to the multiple layers of cloth. A plain black fabric cross is sewn to the front of the coat-of-plates, showing that the wearer is a full brother knight of the Teutonic Order. Sections of the white covering of the coat-of-plates extend downwards at the front and back, but broad gaps are left on each side. A long-sleeved mail hauberk (4) is worn, with integral soft kid-leather mittens, slit across the fingers, but without a mail coif. The hem is slit at the front and back, and leather laces are visible at the wrist of the hauberk, threaded through the mail for tightening. On the knight's left forearm are three small straps and iron buckles used to tighten the lower sleeves of the quilted gambeson worn beneath the mail hauberk. A plain leather sword-belt can be seen attached to the scabbard on the knight's left hip, from which hangs his sword (5); the leather covering of the wooden scabbard was colour-stained and the more decorated uppermost part might be gilded – the lower end of the scabbard is tipped with a gilded bronze chape. Details of the hilt are depicted alongside (6), showing the faceted gilded iron pommel, leather-covered grip, gilded iron quillons, and the lacing system that attached the sword-belt to the scabbard. A long white tunic (7) was worn beneath the mail hauberk, again slit at the front and back of the hem. Mail chausses (8) open down the backs of the legs, where they are closed with leather laces – a sturdy leather sole is sewn to the lowest links at the foot of the mail chausses. The differing patterns of stitching on the thickly quilted cuisses (9), which protected the thighs, knees and upper shins, probably indicate different densities of quilting for flexibility, most notably over the knees. These cuisses are secured with a leather strap and buckle to a waist-belt beneath the tunic. On the feet are worn gilded bronze prick-spurs with leather straps and gilded buckles.

The rear view of the knight shows the separate mail coif worn beneath the arming cap and the leather laces used to tighten it around the head. The upper part of the coat-of-plates goes over the shoulders and then beneath the wrap-around 'sides' before re-emerging as an unplated fabric 'flap' over the buttocks. The plated 'sides' of the coat-of-plates wrap around and are secured with three sets of straps and buckles, the right 'side' overlapping the left beneath these straps. On the backs of his calves can be seen the lacing down the back of the mail chausses, the close-fitting woollen hose worn beneath, and the leather soles sewn into the chausses. On front of the shield that he holds are the arms of Conrad von Thüringen und Hessen, *Hochmeister* of the Teutonic Order from 1239 to 1240. The painted parchment covering goes over an embossed gesso 'lion' to give a slightly three-dimensional image. The unpainted parchment-covered interior of the wooden shield (10), had a system of riveted leather holding straps – the plain leather guige, which suspended the shield over his shoulders, has an iron adjustment buckle.

In 14th-century Germany there was a noticeable development of the great helm. A transitional form of flat-topped helmet (11) had a rigidly attached visor or face-mask. In Germany this style was often worn with a large, slightly quilted, brightly-coloured and sometimes embroidered hat over the top. An early form of great helm (12) did not cover much of the neck, but more protection was offered by the fully developed 13th-century German style of great helm (**13**). The late 13th-century German great helm (**14**) had a top consisting of a single complex-shaped plate. The point is a ventilation hole or plume-holder.

Some examples of 13th-century swords are shown: a typical form of sword from Germany during the first half of the 13th century (**15**); a sword from the third quarter of the 13th century, probably German but found in Scandinavia (**16**); a 13th-century German sword from Leipzig, with a gilded inscription set into the fuller of the blade (**17**); a late 13th-century Italian sword (**18**) of a type which some Teutonic Knights might have adopted during the period when the Order's headquarters were located in Venice; and a mid-13th-century sword-blade with its original long tang, as delivered from the sword-smith and never having had a hilt attached, found in Bohemia but probably made in Germany (**19**).

The flags show some examples of the heraldry of the Teutonic Order: The Banner of the Order of Teutonic Knights (**20**); the banner of the Commander of Königsberg, one of the most important fortresses and garrisons within Teutonic Knights' territory (**21**); the 'Cross of St George' banner under which crusading volunteers from Western Europe served when fighting for the Order of Teutonic Knights (**22**); and the legendary 'banner of the *Hochmeister* of the Teutonic Knights', supposedly used in the Kingdom of Jerusalem during the first decades of the Order's existence (**23**).

C: TEUTONIC KNIGHTS NEGOTIATE THE SURRENDER OF THEIR CONVENT IN ACRE, 1291

The little that is known about what happened to the surviving members of the Order of Teutonic Knights when the last major crusader-held city of Acre fell in 1291 comes from Arab Islamic sources. Having brought 40 knights and about 200 other crusaders to bolster the defences, the Teutonic Knights' *Hochmeister*, Burchard von Schwanden, had left again in 1289, seemingly in disgust at the Order's unwillingness to commit itself wholeheartedly to the Middle Eastern crusade. His deputy, Heinrich von Bouland, was killed early in the siege and consequently command was now in the hands of the German Master, Conrad von Feuchtwangen, who may have come to the city with the 40 knights whom Burchard brought in 1289. Paradoxically, he was one of those most in favour of abandoning the Middle East to concentrate the Teutonic Knights' efforts in the Baltic. Presumably Conrad von Feuchtwangen (**1**) was also the official who negotiated the surrender of the German Order's fortified convent building to Sultan Al-Ashraf's representative Zain al-Din Kitbugha al-Mansuri (**2**) the day after the city of Acre fell to Mamluk assault. Here each senior man is shown with armed attendants, a Teutonic brother knight (**3**) holding the banner of the German Order and himself being equipped with characteristic German arms and armour of the late 13th century. A brother sergeant of the Order (**4**) may come from Lorraine in the east of the German Empire, being armed with a long-hafted guisarme and wearing a thickly quilted gambeson. In this reconstruction the role of intermediary and translator is taken by a priest of the Nestorian Church (**5**). A Mamluk officer (**6**) wears another version of the wood-lined rather than metallic 'hard hat' used by many Mamluks, while a Mongol refugee in the service of the Mamluk Sultanate (**7**) has the full arms and armour which he presumably brought from Central Asia.

The back of an armoured knight on the carved wooden Levitic Pew, Lower Saxony 1360–70. (*In situ* cathedral, Verden)

D: ARMS AND ARMOUR OF THE TEUTONIC KNIGHTS, 14TH CENTURY

This knight wears a one-piece iron bascinet helmet (**1**), which at the front incorporates a turnbuckle above a positioning lug. At the bottom of the helmet vervelles protrude through holes in the leather strip – a coloured cord threaded through the vervelles secures the aventail to the helmet, the round 'toggle' at the end stopping the cord slipping back. A mail aventail with a thick but unseen layer of padding inside covers the sides of his face, his neck and shoulders, and this example also includes an iron nasal protector hanging loose from a flap of mail over the chin. This would be raised and attached to the front of the helmet by the turnbuckle and lug. Over his chest and abdomen is a green-fabric covered coat-of-plates with horizontal rows of iron scales inside, these being secured to the layers of fabric by bronze rivets. Leather edging trims the coat's armholes. The sides of the coat-of-plates wrap around to the back, where they are tightened by two buckled straps, and secured to the back of the shoulders. Three gilded bronze reinforcement rosettes on the chest act as anchorage points for retaining chains with iron bars at the end, which prevent the loss of important articles such as the sword and dagger – the shorter chain on his left chest would 'retain' a great helm when used. Worn beneath the coat-of-plates is a mail haubergeon with three-quarter-length sleeves, and a hem that drops below the coat-of-plates to points at the front and back. Under the haubergeon is worn a (mostly-hidden) thickly quilted gambeson (**2**). Over the thighs and knees is a linen covering of thickly quilted cuisses, large iron poleyns being worn over the knees and secured by buckled straps. The pendant leather elements may have been to attach the poleyns to the greaves, but here the greaves are worn inside the chausses, so their purpose is uncertain. The greaves (**3**) consist of four pieces of shaped iron linked by riveted leather straps – the obvious vertical 'keel' down the front of the mail chausses on the knight's right shin indicates that these rigid greaves are worn underneath. On his mail-protected feet are worn gilded bronze rowell spurs. Buckled to the top of the coat-of-plates are iron shoulder-pieces with gilded decoration around the edges. Shielding his lower forearm is a vambrace consisting of four pieces of iron linked by riveted straps, plus three buckled straps. Over this taper the gauntlets, which consist of thickly padded leather gloves, to which iron plates are riveted on the backs of the wrists, hands and fingers.

In the left and centre views of this figure, details of the reverse-curved, parchment-covered wooden shield can be seen: the front was painted white with a black cross and the interior was unpainted, with three grips, only two of which have adjustment buckles.

The leather sword-belt has large gilded rosette stiffeners, a buckle and buckle-plate. The scabbard suspension system has the sword-belt in two parts (**4**) attached to offset 'rings' on opposite sides of the mount (the gilded bronze locket around the upper part of the scabbard). The wooden scabbard is covered in velvet, with a gilded bronze chape. The broadsword inside has gilded quillons and pommel, and a leather-covered grip, to which the retaining chain is attached. A short strap that loops over the sword-belt attaches to the supporting strap of the dagger sheath (**5**). The sheath, sitting in a leather loop at the end of the supporting strap, is made of dark leather and has a gilded chape. The large basilard dagger (**6**) has a flattened diamond-section blade and its grip is carved from two faceted pieces of horn or wood, riveted to the tang of the blade.

An early 14th-century German sword (**7**) has a plain iron pommel and quillons, and binding around the leather-covered grip to prevent slipping. A leather flap around and over the quillons (**8**) helps to stop rain getting into the scabbard – there is a simple white-and-black cross painted on the flaps. By the late 14th century this German sword (**9**) has a longer, thicker and more slender blade and long 'hand and a half' grip.

On the left view of the figure can be seen the fastenings on the back of the coat-of-plates, and on his head is worn a thickly quilted plain linen-covered 'arming cap' style of coif, which was largely lined with mail. His sword, scabbard, chausses and poleyn straps can be seen more clearly. In the right-hand illustration the knight has donned over his coat-of-plates a tabard-style surcoat of a brother knight of the Order of Teutonic Knights. The surcoat is fringed all round the edges

and opens fully down both sides, but is loosely closed with black laces below the armpit to the waist. The retaining chains from the coat-of-plates emerge through three slits in the chest of the surcoat.

An evolution in the use of the bascinet helmet in Germany should be noted. The early 14th-century bascinet (**10**) does not go far down the sides and back of the neck. It has a moveable visor on two large swivel rivets and the mail aventail is attached in the normal manner over vervelles. A mid-14th-century bascinet (**11**) has a chin and throat protector fastened either to the interior of the helmet or to the mail aventail. Another mid-14th-century bascinet (**12**) has substantial swivel hinges on the sides, here shown with the visor removed by taking out the pins which go through the hinges. The leather strip over the vervelle studs goes right across the brows. This similar Austrian or northern Italian bascinet from the second half of the 14th century (**13**), incorporates an early form of 'dog-faced' visor attached to a single hinge above the brow. A simple form of bascinet without vervelles (**14**), would be worn over a mail coif, and beneath a second, brimmed iron 'war-hat' helmet. The great helm (**15**) was worn over a bascinet, also having a dagged strip of mail attached to its lower interior rim – a white cloth lambrequin is over the helmet, plus a light wooden heraldic crest painted with the arms of the *Hochmeister*. Cords can be seen below the mail attachments, the straps that tighten the helmet in position around the bascinet beneath. A round-topped bascinet (**16**) would be worn beneath the great helm, the position of which is indicated by the tinted area; four iron 'wedges' on the surface of the bascinet would support the great helm. The last example (**17**) shows a late 14th-century 'dog-faced' bascinet with a gilded finial plate at the top. The 'dog-face' is slightly faceted at the sides and is flattened beneath the 'snout' where there are air-holes, plus larger air-holes along the angled edges.

E: TEUTONIC KNIGHTS' RAIDING PARTY IN LITHUANIA IN MID-WINTER, MID-14TH CENTURY

Many attacks carried out by the Teutonic Knights, their supporters and allies in what are now the Baltic States were in effect slave-raiding. Winter was a preferred season because the frozen surfaces of rivers, marshes and even relatively small streams provided solid highways deep into pagan lands. In winter there was often also better visibility because the leaves had fallen in the deciduous forests that characterized this part

Drawing of a scene of combat between Teutonic Knights and pagan Prussians or Lithuanians on a lost carved capital found in the village of Rothof near Malbork castle, 1310–40. (After V. I. Kulakov)

of northern Europe. On the other hand, if the snow was too deep it could form a barrier, while unexpected blizzards might trap a raiding force deep inside unfriendly territory. In this reconstruction of one such typical raid, the Christian force has managed to reach, overrun and burn a small Lithuanian settlement next to a frozen river. They are commanded by a brother knight of the Teutonic Order (1) who is shown in characteristic mid-14th-century arms and armour, though in reality this style of heavy visored bascinet would probably only be worn in full-scale battle. In deep winter the man's substantial white cloak was not just to show that he was a member of the Teutonic Order, but also to keep him warm. The second brother knight (2) braves the weather without a cloak. A brother sergeant or *Halb-bruder* (3) is almost as heavily armoured as the brother knights, though his lower rank is indicated by the grey-covered coat-of-plates of a *Graumäntler*, which also has a T-shaped rather than complete class on the front. The indigenous Prussian auxiliary light cavalryman and guide (4) may be the most important man on this expedition. He is distinguished by his lighter armour, consisting of an iron war-hat over an old-fashioned mail coif, short-sleeved mail hauberk, iron lamellar cuirass laced with rawhide thongs and 'Lithuanian-style' pavise shield. On this raid the brethren of the Teutonic Order are also accompanied by a temporary volunteer from England (5), of which there were many during the 14th century. His armour and costume, though not his large, visored bascinet, are based upon the little-known carved effigy of Sir William de Keynes in the village of Dodford in the English Midlands. The most unusual item is his limited form of 'helmet' with almost circular ear pieces, which has here been interpreted as a leather arming cap. The captured Lithuanians include a local warrior (6) with rudimentary but effective armour, probably imported or captured from the Russians, and several peasants.

F: THE SIEGE OF MARIENBURG CASTLE IN 1410
The major Teutonic Knights' castle of Marienburg was besieged by the victorious Polish-Lithuanian army and some of its allies in the immediate aftermath of the battle of Tannenberg in 1410. The castle's defence was commanded by Heinrich von Plauen, the Teutonic Knights' commander at Schwetz, and his efforts were so successful and so admired that he was subsequently elected as *Hochmeister* of the Order (1410–13). Although the Polish siege was not pressed very vigorously, it did focus on the south-east side of the castle. This appears to have been badly damaged by the enemy's varied siege weapons; nevertheless the attackers failed to breach the outer walls. In our reconstruction of the desultory bombardment, Heinrich von Plauen (1) wears up-to-date armour of the early 15th century, with the glued fabric covering of his cuirass showing the white ground and black cross of the Teutonic Knights. His bascinet helmet is of the type which could have a so-called 'pig-faced' visor attached to an anchorage point above the brow. The brother knight who accompanies him (2) has a bascinet in which the 'pig-faced' visor is attached to swivels on the sides. The white-and-black heraldic 'uniform' which he wears is not permanently attached to the armour, as worn by Von Plauen, but is a separate, close-fitting surcoat. The military engineer (3) who advises on how to counter the enemy's bombardment and repair the damage is protected by an iron war-hat and a thickly padded jupon. The injured man (4) represents one of those Scandinavian knights who volunteered to serve alongside the Teutonic Order for a season's campaigning.

He has removed his armour except for his quilted jupon, which would be worn beneath a full 'white harness' of steel plates, and his characteristically wide-brimmed Scandinavian 'war hat'. Several labourers (5) are operating the sort of late medieval wooden crane which was used to build cathedrals and castles.

G: ARMS AND ARMOUR OF THE TEUTONIC KNIGHTS, SECOND HALF OF THE 15TH CENTURY
This figure's cuirass is largely based upon a bronze statue of Otto IV of Henneberg-Römhild made in 1488 by Peter Vischer the Elder and now in the Collegiate Church at Römhild, in the eastern German region of Thuringia. He wears a salet style of helmet (1) with the bowl and neck extension forged from a single piece, plus a swivelled visor. Over his chin and collar is worn a bevor to protect the front of the neck. This does not go all round and is secured by buckled straps, the front one of which is visible, while the other goes around the back of the neck. One pauldron covers each shoulder (2); the outer elements of each pauldron can slide slightly beneath the wider and single-fluted inner element. In the armpits can be seen pieces of mail attached to the arming jerkin beneath the cuirass. The breastplate has a raised rim around the armholes and a number of raised ridges for added rigidity. The breastplate is attached to the backplate by internal riveted straps on the left side and short external buckled straps on the right side – a lance-rest, shown here in the lowered position, is screwed to the right of the chest. The plackart (3), or additional plate to cover the abdomen, also forms the uppermost lame of the fauld. The plackart goes over the lower part of the breastplate, making the armour double-layered. The lower three riveted lames of the upwards-laminated fauld (4) provide a small degree of flexibility. Two tassets (5) have a small amount of fluting for rigidity, plus a single raised edge towards the groin and inside of the leg.

The upper arms are protected by a partially fluted rerebrace (6); laminated couters with fluted extensions protect the elbows (7); partially fluted vambraces (8) for the lower arms; and gauntlets (9) for the hands, the plates of which are riveted to a thickly padded inner leather glove.

Close-fitting mail 'shorts' and a codpiece protect the unplated area of the groin. The upper iron leg-harness (10) is buckled by the strap around the rear only of the top of the leg. Additional flexibility and comfort is provided by the fact that the uppermost part of the front of the leg harness consists of four upwards-overlapping riveted lames. The poleyn (11), which protects the knee, has wide and fluted 'wings' on the outside of the leg, plus three riveted lames above and three below the knee. The greaves (12) hinge on the outside of the leg and have short buckled straps on the inside. Also two fluted elements protrude over the ankles, and laminated sabatons (13) with fashionably long toes cover the feet, over which might be worn gilded rowel spurs (14). Mail-lined woollen hose were most often worn beneath the leg harness.

Over the fauld at the waist is secured a leather sword-belt consisting of a broader and tight-fitting belt around the waist and a narrower loose-fitting belt drooping down to the scabbard on the left hip, these belts actually being cut from a single piece of leather. A separate narrow leather belt hangs around the fauld and drops towards the right hip, from which the dagger-sheath is suspended. The sword-belt is attached to the velvet-covered scabbard (15) by two offset rings and an updated version of the old system of crossed straps around

The figure in the white surcoat (24) sports half-length sleeves with puffed shoulders and a black cross on the front. Beneath the armour (25) was worn a mail tippet covering neck and shoulders, with a soft white semi-stiffening linen lining of padding. Under this is an arming jacket made of heavy fabric or kid leather, with the mail element that protects the right armpit removed to show the laces, or 'arming points' that hold it. The mail element protecting the left armpit has been included, attached to the arming jacket by pairs of arming points. The sleeves of the arming jacket are slit at the armpits, and down most of the outside of the arms. Here the latter are partially closed with small buttons above the elbows and at the wrists. Mail 'shorts' reaching to just above the knee are donned over hose, and leather shoes are also worn.

H: MEDIEVAL GERMAN COMBAT TRAINING, ACCORDING TO *FECHTBÜCHER*, 'FIGHT BOOKS' AND OTHER SOURCES

(1) Christian Europe's oldest surviving personal combat treatise, the title of which has been lost, dates from the late 13th or early 14th century and was written in Germany, though in Latin. For reasons which are unknown, the two combatants are characterized as 'The Priest' who serves as an expert or instructor, and 'The Scholar' who features as his pupil. The accompanying text to this fencing movement translates as: 'Here the Priest teaches his Student how, after the actions above [where the Priest defends himself from the Student's attack], he should seize the sword and shield. And note that the Priest cannot free himself from such a grip without dropping his sword and shield'.

(2) The *Codex Wallerstein* was written in German in the late 14th or early 15th century. The first half of the surviving text includes detailed accompanying comments but was copied more than half a century after the original text was written. The second part lacks a commentary but the arms and armour of its figures show it to date from the early 15th century. This combat action is based upon an image in the older, second part of the manuscript, and shows two fully armoured men on foot with shields. Both were armed with a short spear and a sword but the man on the right has dropped his spear in favour of his long-sword which, judging by other images in the same part of this book, he thrusts with both hands, the right grasping the hilt while the left grasps the blade about one-third down its length. His shield is also on his lower left arm. The man on the left carries his shield in the same manner but still uses his spear.

(3) This action comes from the first part of the *Codex Wallerstein*, copied in the second half of the 15th century, and shows one of the fencing manoeuvres used when fighting with a heavy, single-edged falchion. The accompanying German text translates as: 'So if anyone strikes downwards at your head, deflect it with your hand halfway along the blade and receive the stroke on the blade as before. Step quickly behind him with your right foot, and put the pommel to his neck, as depicted here, to throw him on his back'.

(4) The best known of medieval German *Fechtbücher*, 'Fight Books' or combat training manuals, was written by Hans Talhoffer in 1467. Though mostly dealing with combat techniques on foot, Talhoffer also included some instructions about fighting on horseback with a variety of weapons. The caption accompanying this manoeuvre merely states that: 'The horseman on the right captures his opponent's sword under his arm'.

Bronze statue of Otto IV of Henneberg-Römhild made by Peter Wischer the Elder, *c.*1488. (*In situ* parish church, Römhild; photograph U. Koch)

the scabbard, which has a long gilded chape at its tip. The figure holds a 'Hand and half' sword with a flattened diamond-section blade, the hilt of which (16) has gilded quillons, a large fluted pommel, and a leather-covered grip with bulges in the middle. The dagger sheath (17) was secured by rawhide thongs around the belt and has an embossed bulge, beneath which the suspension thongs are tied. The dagger (18) has a leather-covered grip, a large gilded pommel and gilded quillons, the latter having extended 'rings' on each side.

Among other weapons available were: the pole-arm (19, and 20 from above) whose iron head has a slender thrusting spike, a thicker horizontal spike, two very short spikes on the side, and a four-pointed 'hammerhead' on the back; the halbard head (21); and the axehead (22) with a multi-spiked hammer at the back.

The exterior of a parchment-covered wooden 'small pavise' type of shield (23) is shown, painted white with a black cross; on the interior cloth-covered, plaited leather grips attach to iron staples nailed to the back of the pavise on each side of the 'keel recess', and a buckled leather carrying guige is secured through iron rings and staples nailed into the back of the pavise.

INDEX

References to illustrations are shown in **bold**. Plates are shown with page and caption locators in brackets.